Hockey for Everybody

Cam Neely's Guide to the Red-Hot Game on Ice

by Cam Neely

with Brian Tarcy

CHANDLER HOUSE PRESS

1998

Hockey for Everybody: Cam Neely's Guide to the Red-Hot Game on Ice

ISBN 1-886284-17-2
Library of Congress Catalog Card Number 98-72599
First Edition
ABCDEFGHIJK

PUBLISHED BY
Chandler House Press
335 Chandler Street
Worcester, MA 01602
USA

PRESIDENT: **Lawrence J. Abramoff**

PUBLISHER/EDITOR-IN-CHIEF: **Richard J. Staron**

VICE PRESIDENT OF SALES: **Irene S. Bergman**

EDITORIAL/PRODUCTION MANAGER: **Jennifer J. Goguen**

EDITOR: **Joan Paterson**

BOOK & COVER DESIGN: **Marshall Henrichs**

COVER AND AUTHOR PHOTOS: **Sports Action, Steve Babineau**

PHOTOGRAPHY CREDITS: All photographs are supplied by Sports Action, Steve Babineau except for the
following appearing on, page 6, Sports Action, Armen James; page 33, Hockey Hall of Fame; page 84,
Gerry Cheevers by Boston Bruins and Mask by Brian Babineau; page 100, Hockey Hall of Fame; 109
top, Hockey Hall of Fame; Player cards on pages 109-110 from the collection of Steve Babineau; page
112, Rice,Hockey Hall of Fame; page 113, Frank King Clancy, Toronto Maple Leafs, Foster Hewitt by
Imperial Oil-Turofsky, Hockey Hall of Fame; page 114, Charlie Conacher, Imperial Oil-Turofsky
Hockey Hall of Fame and Conn Smythe, by Turofsky; page 115, Maurice Richard by David Bier; page
116, Ted Kennedy, by Turofsky; page 117, Ted Lindsey, Imperial Oil-Turofsky, Hockey Hall of Fame;
page 118, Geoffrion by David Bier, Mahovlich, Toronto Maple Leafs; page 119, Plante, Imperial Oil-
Turofsky, Hockey Hall of Fame; page 120, Beliveau, Les Canadiens; page 121, Terry Sawchuk, Imperial
Oil-Turofsky,Hockey Hall of Fame; page 122, Henri Richard, Frank Prazak, Hockey Hall of Fame

Chandler House Press books are available at special discounts for bulk purchases. For more information about how to arrange such purchases, please contact Irene Bergman at Chandler House Press,
335 Chandler Street, Worcester, MA 01602, or call (800) 642-6657, or fax (508) 756-9425, or find us
on the World Wide Web at www.tatnuck.com.

Chandler House Press books are distributed to the trade by
National Book Network, Inc.
4720 Boston Way
Lanham, MD 20706
(800) 462-6420

Contents

About the Authors

CAM NEELY, former all-star right wing with the Boston Bruins, knows all about hockey. Bruins' President and General Manager Harry Sinden once described Cam as, the "quintessential hockey player" and "everything this franchise (Boston) stands for." Neely played in the NHL for 13 years and was with the Boston Bruins for the last 10 years. His career came to an abrupt end in August 1996 when he was diagnosed with a career-ending hip injury. Neely retired, but not without leaving his mark on the hockey world with 726 games played, 395 goals, 299 assists, 694 total points and 1,256 penalties in minutes. Cam was the perfect hockey player, a blend of toughness, intimidation, and scoring touch. He became the league's first player to be called a "power forward."

As one of the league's top combinations of finesse and hard-nosed hockey, Cam Neely was only the second player in Boston Bruins history to record back-to-back 50-goal seasons. He had his third 50-goal season in 1993–94 and finished the lockout-shortened 1994–95 season with 27 goals in 42 games.

Cam accomplished 14 career hat tricks and for many years led the Bruins in goal scoring. Cam also shares the NHL single season playoff record for the most power play goals. A recipient of many honors and awards in the hockey world, he was named to *The Sporting News* All-Star First Team in 1987–88 and the Second Team in 1989–90 and 1990–91. He also played on the NHL All-Star Teams in 1987–88, 1989–90, 1990–91, 1993–94, and 1995–96. In 1994, Cam won the NHL Bill Masterton Trophy for the player who best exemplified the qualities of perseverance, sportsmanship, and dedication to hockey.

In addition to his impressive record on the ice, Cam engages in a range of activities and interests off the ice. He is one of the most visible professional athletes in the Boston area, making many appearances on behalf of charitable organizations. Most of his efforts are now dedicated toward The Cam Neely Foundation, a tax-exempt charitable foundation where he serves as president.

On August 25, 1997, The Cam Neely Foundation opened the doors to The Neely House —a home away from home for pediatric and adult cancer patients and their families while the patient is undergoing treatment at New England Medical Center in Boston. Located on the grounds of New England Medical Center, it is a refuge for families. Future plans for the Neely Foundation include expansion of the existing Neely House, development and support of a cancer research laboratory, and other educational programs related to cancer. The Foundation and its work was featured on *The Maury Povich Show.*

Aside from his work with the Foundation, Cam has appeared in two motion pictures, *Dumb and Dumber* and *Mighty Ducks II* and is featured in many commercials that air nationwide. He has also guest-starred on the nationally televised show *Beverly Hills 90210.*

Brian Tarcy is a freelance writer and book developer living in Falmouth, Massachusetts. He is the author or co-author of eight books, including a collaboration with ESPN analyst and Super Bowl champion quarterback Joe Theismann called *The Complete Idiot's Guide to Understanding Football Like a Pro* (Alpha Books). Tarcy has also written for several magazines and newspapers and is currently a Cape Cod correspondent for *The Boston Globe*. He has a bachelor's degree in journalism from Ohio University.

 # FOREWORD I

Cam Neely epitomized talent, wisdom, and drive during his great but injury-shortened career. He was a prolific goal scorer who played hockey the way hockey is supposed to be played—he played all out. He played smart and he played to win. And now, Cam has delivered the goods in book form the way he used to deliver on the ice.

Cam knows the modern game. When I played, hockey was just entering major league expansion and international play and we were all beginning to see what lay in store. Clearly, the result of those two events is today's game: a hybrid of European skating and passing with the relentless power of the North American style. In the modern game of hockey, Cam Neely became a star—the prototype power forward. He epitomized strength, speed, knowledge, and willpower. Teams now talk about trying to get a player like Cam Neely.

Cam combined speed with power in his game. He had a knack for finding the net and scored 50 goals three times during his career. In 1994, he scored 50 goals in his first 44 games. Cam Neely at his best was among the very best ever!

Cam could electrify NHL crowds with his power and speed. He jolted many players with his devastating body checks. But most of all, on the ice Cam played smart.

There are no finer human beings around than Cam Neely. He is a class individual who gave his all on the ice and continues to give his all to his community, especially with his efforts to create The Neely House, a place for families of cancer patients to stay while their relatives are being treated in Boston.

I am proud to know Cam Neely and thrilled that he has put his hockey knowledge on paper. Once again, Cam Neely scores!

Bobby Orr

 **FOREWORD II**

Over the course of almost 45 years associated in one form or another with professional hockey—more years than I care to remember—I have been fortunate to both play with and see many outstanding right wingers: Gordie Howe, Terry O'Reilly, Johnny "Pie" McKenzie, Vic Stasiuk, and Ken Hodge come to mind. So do the ones I sometimes found myself matched against: Rocket Richard, Andy Bathgate, Boom Boom Geoffrion, Yvon Cournoyer, and Rod Gilbert, to mention a few.

Others have come along as shining stars: Guy Lafleur, Brett Hull, Mike Bossy, Jari Kurri, and more recently Jaromir Jagr and Teemu Selanne. Yet, when he was at the top of his game, none has been more effective and meant more to his team on the ice than Cam Neely.

When you think of power forwards during the last 20 years, Cam comes to mind. With his tremendous upper body strength, he'd go into a corner and you knew he'd come out with the puck. He would drive to the net and be next to impossible to knock off of his feet, despite the abuse he received. Scoring 50 goals during 49 games during the 1993–94 season (all were scored in his first 44 games) while making a remarkable comeback from a serious upper leg injury was one of the most determined accomplishments by a player in NHL history!

Off the ice, few realized the personal tragedy he went through, first losing his mom to cancer and then his good-natured dad, who was Cam's best friend as well as his father. And what did Cam do when his playing career was over? He gave something back, overseeing what is now The Neely House, a place to stay for families who have children in the hospital with serious illnesses. One less worry for the families, thanks to Cam.

It's unfortunate Cam Neely's career with the Bruins was cut short. But at least we got to see him at his best, and we still get to see him at his best in the community. Cam's a winner who never quits!

JOHN BUCYK

 # *INTRODUCTION*

Out in western Canada where I grew up, all the boys played hockey. It's what we did, and from what I understand, it's what the kids in eastern Canada and a good part of the northern United States did too. Later, we learned that the kids in Europe were also playing the red-hot game on ice.

When I retired from the Boston Bruins earlier than I wanted to, due to an injury, I took a deep breath and looked around. I examined the game that I have loved my entire life and realized how much it grew during the span of my 13-year career.

Despite my retirement, I knew I still had something to contribute. During my career, I was privileged to play with and against some great players. I learned a lot and decided to write this book to share that knowledge and to share my love of hockey.

This is a guide to the game of hockey. My approach is simple: I first teach you about the game itself, the rules and equipment. And then I move into the strategies of the game and the makeup of professional hockey. You will also learn a little about the great players from the past and the present. I conclude with some basic teaching chapters for hockey players, focusing especially on the mental approach all players should bring to the game. This book is my way of saying simply this: Hey, this is hockey.

I hope you enjoy playing the game of hockey and participating as a fan. I hope you enjoy reading this book as much as I enjoyed writing it. I bet you will...after all, the subject is hockey. So follow me. Lace 'em up or grab a program. Let's go check out the ice!

Cam Neely

The Basics of the Game

Hockey is majestic and it is basic: a game that is a combination of speed, power, and grace and, most of all, fun. It is played at the highest level of professional sporting competition and it is the most exciting sport of all for everyone who has watched a game. Hockey rules!

In the first part of the book, you will find a primer on the game to teach you about the rink, the equipment, and the rules. All the penalties are covered in this part of the book as well. It's time to drop the puck!

Hockey Rules!
Why the Game Is Great

hen the great cleft-chinned masters of weighty subjects write the history of western civilization, chances are they will give hockey short shrift. But as every fan knows, hockey prevented World War III.

In 1980 the Soviet Union was battling the United States for world dominance. Both countries had really big guns. And both had Olympic hockey teams. The United States had bigger guns, but everyone believed (including folks in America) that the Soviet Union had a superior hockey team.

During the 1980 Winter Olympics in Lake Placid, New York, the older and clearly professional team from the Soviet Union lost to a bunch of amateur kids from the United States. A few years later, the Soviet Union collapsed. A coincidence? Ask a hockey fan.

Now some of the best players in the National Hockey League (NHL) are from the old Soviet Union, and there is peace and prosperity in almost the entire hockey-playing world. Hockey—it rules!

ORIGINS OF HOCKEY

Hockey has exploded across North America. Originating in Europe as a sort of field hockey more than 500 years ago, the game evolved onto ice because, presumably, someone wanted to play in the winter.

By the time the NHL was born in 1917, hockey games were events of epic proportions in Canada. In his 1967 book, *The Lively World of Hockey, A History of the National Hockey League* (New American Library), Canadian Sportscaster Brian McFarlane described the early years of the league this way:

"...the NHL soon caught the fancy of fans, despite growing pains that produced rowdies, ringers, and riots. Skulls were cracked and blood flowed with shocking regularity. Games were played in drafty barn-like arenas, under poor lighting, and on ice that might be rock-hard or soft as putty, even deliberately salted to slow down a fast team.

"The fans loved it," continued McFarlane. "They bundled up and stood in sub-zero temperatures to curse and cheer alternately as two teams from rival cities clashed on the ice. Overcoat pockets often concealed rotten fruit and vegetables to be hurled at officials and opposing players when the home team was taking the worst of it. The post-game battles between rival factions in local bars were often far more spectacular than the donnybrooks on the ice."

Hockey is now a sport of multimillion–dollar athletes playing in spectacular new arenas before sellout crowds of Sunbelt Americans. But the passion is still there, even if there isn't as much rotten fruit and vegetables. And hockey is still hockey, a primitive and intellectual game of quick reactions. It's just that more people "get it" now. That's the point of this book—to help you "get it"—because hockey is the best sport on earth.

 ## THE PERFECT MIX

Speed. Power. Grace. Athleticism. Hockey roars like a Neanderthal and then instantaneously challenges your brain's ability to comprehend a thousand things at once: the turn of a skate, the flick of a wrist, or the ferocious slam of a *body check*—a hit that one player puts on another player's body.

The players have sticks, skates, blades, colorful uniforms, and varied styles and degrees of talent. One player on a team is a goalie who stands in front of the net and stops the puck. Look, it's not my right as a human being to question any other person's mental stability but, this hard rubber puck aimed directly at a goalie can fly faster than 100 mph! Sure, he has pads and a mask. So what?

Hockey is thrilling for a million different reasons, but the mix of all of them is what creates the magic of the game. Hockey is a spectacle with a beautiful and often dramatic flow. You don't know what's going to happen next. If you're watching a game and turn your head, you might miss a body check or a goal. Hockey is excitement. And, oh yeah, it all happens on ice.

The Majesty of Speed, Power, and Grace

Every goal is a great goal. After all, no one asks how, the question is how *many*. Nevertheless, some goals are clearly prettier than others. One of the beautiful things about hockey is that every opportunity to score offers a chance for something new and different. As beauty is in the eye of the beholder, what's your preference?

Speed: Sometimes you see a great passing play—bing, bing, bing—and the puck is in the net. It's like watching the laws of physics in high-speed action. The puck bouncing from stick to stick through a maze of players can be so quick that hockey can look like a game of full-contact billiards.

Power: Sometimes a goal is the result of a huge shot—something in warp speed with afterburners that leaves the goalie wondering what has just happened.

Grace: Another special part of hockey involves a great skater who is so deft with his skates and stick that he fakes out his defender with a quick *deek*,

Hockey is full of majesty.

leaving the defender lurching one way while the offensive player drives toward the goalie. A deek is a tactical move used on another player. When a defender is the victim of a deek, players say: He was deeked out of his jockstrap.

The best part of a deek is the finish, when a player drives on the goalie and fakes him out. A dip, a juke, a backhand, a forehand, and suddenly the war of nerves is over. He shoots, he scores!

Athleticism

Hockey is a game of energy bursts. But the flow is constant and the energy level is always at the highest. How is this possible? Substitutions—more on how this works in Chapter 2.

Hockey allows players to go on and off the ice as often as they want. A typical forward plays an average of 45 seconds at a time, while a typical defenseman (because he doesn't have as far to skate) plays about twice as long at any one time. Although this may seem like a short period of time, the energy expended while on the ice is almost total. A player will come back to the bench at the end of a shift breathing hard and physically drained. Of course, these athletes are so well conditioned that they are able to recover within a minute and get back on the ice to attack again.

Hockey is an anaerobic sport and players must train year round to stay in shape. This is not a minor kind of athleticism. Players know the type of special athlete it takes to participate at the highest levels of hockey. The energy expended at any level of hockey is outrageous. Players who compete against the best are the best and the degree of skill on display on a nightly basis in the NHL is mind-boggling. Stick handlers and intimidators, skaters and hitters, passers and thieves—a world of personalities on emotional and physical display as they fly over the ice with power and grace.

PHYSICAL AND MENTAL TOUGHNESS

Hockey is no mere game of finesse. It can be brutally tough—more a war of muscle and willpower than of nerves. Goals in hockey are not always the result of a great offensive play. Often, a goal is the result of a mistake. The fascinating part about this in-your-face game is its subtlety. And yet the subtlety can be obvious, as in the case of intimidation. When a player makes his physical presence felt, the entire opposing team reacts in ways that only the laws of physics can explain. For every action, there is a reaction, and for every hit, there is a hurting. When players know there is a hurting awaiting, they think a little longer before heading in to take it. Or they try and figure out a way to get around it. Intimidation is a mental factor.

Hockey is intellectual in that it is analytical, using angles, hits, fakes, and positioning. With an unseen calculator, fans and players alike are constantly evaluating as the action progresses.

And then, of course, there is hockey's pure willpower and emotion. During a game, players never stop except to rest on the bench. Although in skating—as in bicycling, for example—there is gliding, there is usually never anything less than 1 million percent effort. A forward (more on positions in chapters 2, 4-7) is on the ice for 30 to 45 seconds at a time. This is not about coasting—it is about effort. Bring the puck up the ice. Pass, move, catch, shoot, and then attack for the rebound. Angles and energy. Players rev it as high as it goes and then fly like maniacs and bang like bumper cars on the ice. Hockey roars.

 ## TEAMWORK

Tight passing exemplifies teamwork in hockey but is not the only kind of teamwork. There is also the teamwork of a hitter and a skater working together to intimidate an opponent while getting the puck in the hands of the skater. The playmaker and the scorer—so perfectly tuned each can read the other's eyes.

Two or more players who work well together are fun to watch. When they are on the ice, they can appear magical. They know each other so well that they not only know the designated way to try and do something, they also know each other's strengths and are able to react accordingly. The chemistry is hard to explain but very noticeable. After all, teams win championships, not individuals.

 ## ALTERCATIONS

Hockey is a physical game and hitting is a big part of it. Hockey players carry sticks, which they sometimes use as swords. Inevitably, as players travel at phenomenal speeds and crash into each other while chasing a small round disk with their sticks, there will be confrontation. And hockey players are macho athletes who do not back down easily. Some actually thrill in the fight. Hit me again. It hurts good, so take that! Fights—one of the oldest jokes around goes: I went to a fight last night and a hockey game broke out.

The NHL is rightfully trying to stop fighting to some extent, but I believe that, in this raw and primitive sport, players are sometimes going to want to go at it. The referees usually let them go at it until they tire out. It usually doesn't take too long and often not much happens. Mostly they throw down their gloves and pummel each other's pads. Throwing down the gloves is what the players do before they fight so that they can get a better hit in—one that hurts. And they sometimes hit more than pads.

Remember, these guys are used to playing in 45-second spurts, so a fight will not usually last too long. Of course, it can be 45 seconds of carnage. Fights are part of the game and I believe fighting should not be taken out of hockey totally.

THERE IS HOCKEY BECAUSE THERE IS ICE

Think about it. You fall on ice; you slide on ice; it is cold and hard and slippery and not designed for human navigation, or at least it wasn't until some genius figured out that a thin blade of metal sharpened just right could cut a swath through it. This game-on-the-rocks is faster than all others because it is played on ice. Some skaters can go faster than 30 mph on the ice. The game is especially fast when the Zamboni has just put down a fresh layer of ice.

A Zamboni is a big vehicle used in hockey rinks to clean the ice and lay down a new layer of ice. It works by first scraping off the layer of flecked ice that is created by skate blades. The four-wheel drive vehicle then lays down a thin layer of water from the back of the machine that quickly freezes into a smooth surface. At the end of each period of a game, the Zamboni comes out and  **cleans the ice. The machine is an outgrowth of a successful experiment by a California rink operator, Frank Zamboni, who used a tractor to scrape the ice.**

Round Corners Mean No Out of Bounds

Skaters can go fast, but they can't go on forever. Hockey is a game of short bursts because there is a boundary that separates the ice from the rest of the world. If you want to go out of bounds in hockey, you have to leap over a wall. Like the ancient Romans in the Coliseum—players are closed in with the lion. If you are carrying the puck and someone is going to hit you, you cannot go out of bounds to avoid the hit. Mr. Player, meet Mr. Wall. Hockey is such a flowing game, there are no hard corners—only rounded edges.

Pucks, Skates, and Sticks

I once heard a comedian describe hockey players as "absurd. They use sticks for swords and they walk around with knives on the bottom of their feet." The comedian is right, of course. Hockey can appear absurd. It's also fun to play, fun to watch, and a perfect game of speed and power.

Hockey equipment is designed to be used on ice (Chapter 3 goes into more detail on equipment). For now, keep in mind that hockey is a fast game in which there are more skills than skating and stickhandling. But, these two skills are the most important.

Basic Equipment.

Pucks: The puck is the center of attention. For anyone who didn't grow up with hockey, it's the "ball" of the game.

Skates: Skates are what players put on their feet and use to move around the ice. Anybody who has tried to skate realizes that it's not really an easy thing to do unless you've grown up doing it. Players like to tie their skates up differently. Some like them loose, some like them tight, and some like them so stiff and tight that they even put tape around them. It is a matter of personal preference. I will discuss skates and equipment in depth in Chapter 3.

Sticks: Sticks are what players use to move the puck around the ice. Some sticks are long, some are short. Some are curved one way, some curved another—depending, of course, on which hand you use to shoot. A player who puts his right hand lower on the stick shoots with his right, while a player who puts his left hand lower on the stick shoots with his left. Some sticks are made of wood with fiberglass, and some are constructed of aluminum with fiberglass or wood. Sticks are an extension of a player's arms and the player has to feel comfortable for the stick to work for him. When it does, there is beauty and grace as a good skater and stickhandler moves up the ice with the puck.

 ## HOW TO WIN—SIMPLE VERSION

Each team of five players plus a goaltender tries to send the puck into a net (called a goal) defended by the other team. Every time the puck goes in the net, the team not defending that net gets one goal. The game is 60 minutes long, divided into three 20-minute periods. At the end of the game, whichever team has the most goals wins.

Games can be tied. In the NHL, a tie results in a five-minute sudden death overtime period. The first team that scores wins. If no team wins at the end of overtime, the game ends in a tie. However, in the playoffs, the overtime period is a full 20 minutes. If neither team wins, the teams keep playing overtime periods until one team wins. In the playoffs, there are no ties. One team must win.

TIME TO LACE 'EM UP

What do you say? Come on along and I'll teach you about the fastest and greatest game around. If you are a young player, I will teach you how to become a better player. If you are a fan, I will teach you the intricacies of this sport. You don't even need a helmet or pads. Just bring your enthusiasm.

The Object of the Game

n first look, hockey is a simple game: Score more goals than your opponent and win the game. Sending the puck into the opposing team's net scores goals.

On second look, hockey is still a pretty simple game: Each team has five players and a goaltender, and each player has a hockey stick, although goaltenders have a stick and a special glove (more on goaltenders in Chapter 7). As the puck slides across the ice, teammates work together to stop the other team from scoring and to score goals for their team.

THE LIFE OF A PUCK

The puck is made of vulcanized rubber—doesn't that sound cool? It is 1 inch thick by 3 inches in diameter and weighs between 5 1/2 and 6 ounces. For all games, the supply of pucks must be frozen. The home team supplies the pucks.

The puck is always the center of attention in hockey.

Pucks are made of hard rubber and would bounce on the ice if they were not frozen. When a puck moves down the ice, a player isn't dribbling it—he or she is sliding it. At every game, a bucket of pucks is kept on ice because, when a puck flies into the stands, it belongs to the lucky fan who recovers it.

100 Miles Per Hour

It is exciting to watch a hockey puck travel at 100 miles per hour. And it is fun to create that rate of speed. But it is not fun to catch a puck in the body. That's the life of a puck. It glides and slides and, in the right hands, a puck dances on a stick until it flies like a missile with a guidance system.

Zero Miles Per Hour

Ice surfaces aren't perfect. If the Zamboni puts down too much water, the puck will stick. A player can skate along and then suddenly won't have the puck because it has stopped dead in a puddle. Inevitably, as play goes along, the ice will get chewed up by all the skating and will actually turn into snow, which slows play. Goalies sometimes ask for a squeegee for the puddles and a shovel for the snow around the net.

 ## HOCKEY RINKS

Hockey is a game that was once played on frozen ponds and lakes. It still is by kids in colder climates. Over the past century, however, hockey has grown into a huge business played in multimillion-dollar arenas with ice surfaces that are not at the mercy of the elements. Instead, the ice is smooth and is supposed to be in the same condition for every game. A Zamboni takes care of the ice (see Chapter 1). Through the years and across the world, ice surfaces have come in many different sizes. This accounts for the variety of styles of play in different parts of the world.

The official ice size now in the NHL is 200 feet long by 85 feet wide and, as you learned in Chapter 1, the corners are rounded. In the old days in the NHL (when I played), there were a few rinks that were smaller than the size now considered regulation. The reason was that some of these buildings (including the Boston Garden where I played) were built decades before there was a standard-size rink. The rink at the Boston Garden was only 191 feet by 83 feet. The Garden has since been replaced by the Fleet Center, which has a standard-size rink.

Rink size makes a difference. A bigger rink means there is more room to skate. Players who play on a bigger rink find their skating skills are more important, whereas those who play on smaller rinks play a tougher, banging style of hockey that relies a little more on strength and hitting. European rinks (and those used in the Olympics) are even bigger—200 feet by 100 feet—making skating skills even more important. There are now many NHL players from Europe noted for their skating and puck-handling skills.

A hockey rink looks like this:

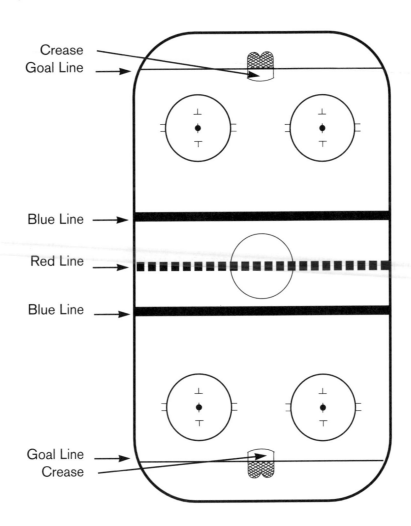

Red and Blue Lines

The idea of hockey is to create an exciting, fast-moving game that thrives on quick, slick passing, hard hitting, and precise movements. While hockey is about action and shooting the puck, the red and blue lines on the ice ensure that the puck moves from player to player without exceedingly long passes.

Here is what the red and blue lines signify:

- The Red Line is a one-foot-wide line that dissects the middle of the ice surface, running the width of the ice from board to board. This area is also called *center ice*.

- There are two one-foot-wide Blue Lines 60 feet from each goal, running the width of the ice from board to board.

- There is a thin two-inch-wide red line (this is not "the Red Line") that is the goal line, running the width of the ice from board to board.

These lines are put on the ice with paint and then covered with thin layers of ice (more on the rules revolving around these lines in Chapter 3).

Zones

The area from the Blue Line back to a team's defensive goal is called their defensive zone. Alternately, it is called the other team's attacking zone. The area between the Blue Lines is called the neutral zone.

The Goal

The goal is a simple rectangle, framed by metal posts and backed by a sort of fishing net. Inside the goal is the Holy Grail of Gametime, the key to progress. Get the puck in your opponent's goal and you have scored ONE. This is a great feeling when you are on offense.

If, however, the other team has the puck and is approaching your goal, defend it at all costs. In that situation, the goal is your flag. This simple rectangle is everything—it holds the keys to both heaven and hell in hockey.

The goal is 6 feet wide by 4 feet high. If the puck goes completely over the goal line (landing usually, but not always, in the net) a goal is scored. It cannot be *deliberately* batted in with any part of the body or skate, although it can get knocked in. When one team scores, the other team gives up a score. Ecstasy and agony in an instant! That's the result of a goal in hockey.

The Crease

There is a semicircular crease in front of each goal. This crease belongs to the goalie and the defensemen on his team as well as his offensive teammates— a center and two forwards—if they wander back there.

Offensive players may skate through the crease if they have no contact with anyone. But, if they are in the crease and a goal is scored, the goal is disallowed. If an offensive player is in the crease (even just his skate blade) when his team scores a goal, the goal will be disallowed. If a player was pushed or held in the crease, the referee can allow the goal. I have seen some goals disallowed that made me shake my head. Sometimes, it seems that the player in the crease had no impact whatsoever on the play. But at least the rule is clear to everyone, a non-judgmental call. Personally, I don't like this rule; I would prefer a judgmental call based on whether there is interference with the goalie. If just the toe of your skate is in the crease, it shouldn't disallow a goal.

Face-Off Circles

There are five red circles on the ice. These are face-off circles. The referee sometimes drops the puck in these circles between a player from each team. The reason is to restart play after a lost puck, an infraction, or any stoppage of play, i.e., when a goalie makes a save and covers the puck. When the infraction occurs (or when a puck is lost) near a face-off circle, the puck is dropped in that circle. When the puck is dropped between two players, it is called a face-off. Thus, the name "face-off circles."

One face-off circle is in the middle of the ice. This is used for face-offs at the beginning of the game and at the beginning of each period. In addition, this is where a face-off is held after a goal is scored by either team.

Face-Off Spots

Things happen all over the ice, so there are also four face-off spots in the neutral zone, just inside the Blue Lines. There are no circles around them. Mainly, this is where a face-off occurs when an offsides is called.

 **TIME**

The game is 60 minutes long, divided into three 20-minute periods. (In lower levels, games can be divided into periods of 15, 12, or 10 minutes, or even shorter.) If there is a whistle to stop the play, the clock will stop running.

If the game is tied after the 60 minutes, there is a five-minute sudden death overtime. The first team to score during that five minutes wins the game. If neither team scores, the game ends in a tie. In the playoffs, however, there are no ties. If a playoff game is tied after 60 minutes, there is a 20-minute sudden death overtime. If that overtime ends in a tie, the game continues with 20-minute overtimes until one team scores.

 REFEREES AND LINESMEN: KEEPING ORDER

It is not an easy job to be the judge of a hockey game. After all, hockey is a fast, furious game. Those in charge need to act with authority. There are three policemen on the ice—one referee and two linesmen—who are charged with keeping order, handling face-offs, and calling penalties. Their roles are very similar.

The *referee* has the final word on all goals or calls (although he can be overruled by the *video replay judge*). The referee drops the puck at center ice to start all periods.

Linesmen can also call penalties, but only major penalties—this rarely happens. Linesmen are responsible for all face-offs that do not occur at center ice.

Sometimes there are center ice face-offs that do not occur after a goal. Linesmen also drop the puck on these face-offs.

In addition, there is a *goal judge* at each end of the rink who sits in a booth in the first row behind the boards directly behind the goalie. When he sees that the puck has crossed the goal line, he flips a switch to turn on a green light at that end of the rink. This light is on the top of the Plexiglas behind the goalie and above the goal judge's head. A *video goal judge* watches a video of controversial goals to make a final decision on goals.

 ## THE PLAYERS: A PRIMER

In many ways the alignment of the players is like the alignment of a military force: Start with a strategy and then react to the situation. The rules are simple. Each team has 20 players: 12 forwards (centers and wingers); 6 defensemen; and 2 goalies. At any one time, five players and one goalie are allowed on the ice, unless there is a penalty (more on this in Chapter 3). Here is the general alignment that all teams use:

- one goalie
- two defensemen—a left defenseman and a right defenseman
- one center
- two wingers (or wings)—a left-winger and a right-winger

This is how players are aligned to start a game.

That's where they start. But a game flows and moves and players glide all over the ice in pursuit of the puck as they attack and defend goals. Players stay in zones that are flexible in their makeup, depending on the game situation. This is another way to say that hockey is fast and unpredictable. Here are the player positions:

- *Goalie.* Stays inside the crease and shifts from pole to pole to cut the angle for the shooter (more in Chapter 7).

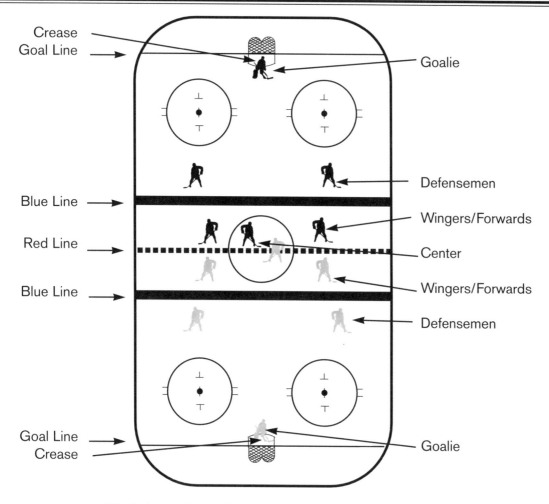

Crease
Goal Line
Blue Line
Red Line
Blue Line
Goal Line
Crease

Goalie
Defensemen
Wingers/Forwards
Center
Wingers/Forwards
Defensemen
Goalie

This is how players line up at the beginning of the game.

- **Defensemen.** At least one will lay back to prevent a breakaway. Sometimes a defenseman will be offensive-minded, able to attack the goal and increase the odds for the offense by one (more on this in Chapter 5).
- **Center.** Takes most face-offs. In the defensive zone, the center goes into the corners to help defensemen. In the offensive zone, the center has freedom to create (more in Chapter 4).
- **Wingers.** Both sides are set up to score, sometimes with power and sometimes with speed and finesse. Wingers depend a lot on the mix with each other and with the center (more in Chapter 4).

LINES, PAIRS, AND STRATEGIES

A *line* consists of a center and two wingers. A *pair* of defensemen is exactly that—a pair of defensemen. Generally, lines play together and pairs of defensemen play together. It creates cohesiveness and teamwork.

In order to understand *strategy,* it is first important to understand that different players bring different skill sets and levels to the same position. Here are some examples:

- A defenseman could be an offensive-defenseman (possessing above-average offensive skills for a defenseman) and is able to help on offensive rushes.
- Wingers and centers can be defensive-minded, concentrating more on defense—prevent everything—than offense.
- Centers should all be able to pass accurately from the forehand and the backhand.
- Wingers can be scorers or *plumbers,* a term meaning someone who has difficulty scoring.

On defense, teams have certain pairings that they prefer. They will have either two defensive-minded defensemen together or one offensive-minded defenseman with one defensive-minded defenseman. Never sacrifice defense completely. A defenseman who can rush on offense and can help out the center and wingers is invaluable. Remember, hockey is a numbers game. One extra player on offense helps a lot.

Of course, it often comes down to matchups. What players did the other coach put on the ice? Strategies and matchups are pretty straightforward. Some players rely more on speed and some more on strength. The idea is to create a matchup that you think gives you an advantage.

Some teams put their best defensive players against the other team's best offensive players. Each coach does it differently, but I personally like to see the offensive big guns go at each other. Offense against offense. Star against star. That's hockey at its best. You see more offensive play that way, but players still take great pride in their defense, which doesn't completely disappear. It is exciting to see scorers and playmakers play together and against each other. On the other hand, if you put in your best defensive forwards against the other team's best defensive forwards, offense will suffer. Every player and every skill serve a purpose: toughness, speed, teamwork, passing, hitting. Because of the pure gung-ho athleticism of hockey, numerous substitutions are required. Thus, there are numerous strategies for numerous situations. And remember, there is never a set, static situation in hockey. The game flows, and so does the strategy.

LINES AND SHIFTS: WHEW! THAT'S TIRING

Hockey requires a ridiculous amount of energy—everything you have plus a whole bunch more. You go so hard and fast and furious and with such emotional and adrenaline energy that you cannot stay on the ice for a long time. It is impossible to keep up with a fresh player if you are not fresh yourself.

Players do not stay on the ice for the entire game. Instead, they go out for shifts of between 45 seconds and 2 minutes. Forwards and centers, who move about the ice a lot, play an average of 45 seconds at a time, while defensemen usually are on the ice longer and can play up to 2 minutes at a time. Remember, hockey is a very anaerobic sport. Rarely will a player return to the bench after his shift without sucking wind from playing so hard.

Goaltenders stay in the entire time unless they are playing poorly or become injured. If either of those situations occurs, the coach replaces the goalie with the backup goalie.

Changing on the Fly

Forty-five seconds is not a lot of time, unless you spend it on the ice. For the coach, coordinating changes is an art form that requires concentration and cooperation from all players.

The purpose of a change is simple: to replace tired players with fresh players without disrupting your chances to score. Changes are also made for line matchups. Coaches like to put certain players against others. Players can sometimes be on the ice for only seconds before they are told to change. The clock doesn't always stop to give a coach that opportunity, so players must sometimes change during the action, called *changing on the fly*. Changes do not occur at any precise instant. Instead, they occur within the context of the flow of the game, whenever a team decides it can make a quick change and the changing player will not figure in what happens during the next few seconds.

Rarely will you change if the other team has control of the puck. That is a dangerous time to change. A good strategy, if you are tired, is to get the puck to the Red Line and dump it deep into your opponents' zone. Then all three players from your line will go to the bench. The other team has to go 100 feet to chase the puck. This gives your players time to get to the bench and the new players time to get in and make sure nothing happens to hurt them defensively. That's always the first priority.

Lines often, but not always, will change together. Sometimes the coach will yell, "Hey, change!" and then the designated player comes off the ice. Or, when a coach wants a line change, he may have a signal, such as having the spare goalie put his glove over the boards. When a change does occur, the new player cannot enter the ice until the player who is leaving is within five feet of the bench.

Who Is Up?

The question comes all game long. *Who's up?* If you are up, you are next in line to go in. Rotations occur and lines play together and apart, at the whim of the coach. He uses what he thinks will work based on matchups, tendencies, recent history, and gut feeling. Sometimes he just has a feeling that three players will play well together. In the end, it always depends on the three players. So if you are up, you had better be ready.

Changing When Time Stops

When the clock is stopped, the visiting team makes line changes first and is given about 10 to 15 seconds. Then the referee signals for the home team to make changes. This gives the home team a chance to make changes based on strategy and matchups. Of course, as soon as play begins, the visiting team can make changes on the fly to adjust to the home team's line changes.

 ## THE NUMBERS GAME

A core strategy of hockey is quite elementary: The race up and down the ice is often a numbers game. If your team can get more players up the ice on offense than the other team can get back in time on defense, your team has a distinct advantage. They can't cover everybody. It's simple math:

- One can't cover two.
- Two can't cover three.
- Three can't cover four.
- Four can't cover five.

Elementary. And in the NHL, it is crucial because the skills of the shooters are well developed. A wide-open opponent with the puck is not a welcome sight for a goaltender. On the other hand, I have sometimes been that player with the puck—then it's fun!

Equipment, Rules, and Penalties

ockey hurts. Hockey as a game has many opportunities to put a pounding on your body so that you can remember it. And precisely because hockey hurts, players wear standard equipment. In addition, there are rules and there are penalties for breaking the rules. Hockey is fast and quick and there are also rules about where and when the puck can be passed and where and when players can move to the offensive end of the ice.

Hockey is simple and specific: There are 93 rules in the NHL rulebook. I will cover the most common ones in this book. The purpose of the equipment and the rules is to promote safety, fairness, and maximum excitement.

EQUIPMENT

A hockey player is dressed to the nines—in protective gear, that is. The equipment for one player can cost $400 or more. A player's mode of protection, developed over the years, is designed to prevent injuries while allowing maximum mobility on the ice. Mobility may at first appear to be difficult, given the bulky look of hockey equipment. But watch a real hockey player moving easily over the ice and you will see that it is easy to adjust. The protective gear looks natural on hockey players.

Skates

It all starts with skating. Thus, it all starts with skates—the mode of transportation for hockey players. The romantic image of hockey skates as the leather boots of old is just that, a romantic image. Hockey boots are now wonders of technology, a mix of leather, plastic, and other materials to give maximum comfort and support.

The skate blades are shaped with an indentation running through the middle, so that each edge is sharp.

Skates are high-tech wonders. When the blades are sharpened, the indentation in the middle can be made more or less hollow, as illustrated in this enlarged, head-on view of a skate blade. A more hollow indentation gives the player more maneuverability but less stability.

The inside of the blade's indentation is called the hollow. The deeper the hollow, the easier it is to maneuver. A hollow that is not as deep gives more stability. Offensive skaters usually prefer a deeper hollow; defensive players typically like a flatter blade.

Hockey players should also consider the radius of the skate blade; in other words, how much of the blade actually touches the ice. Some skate blades are curved so that there is less of the skate on the ice, while other blades are not curved nearly as much. Offensive players who rely on their skating ability usually like less of the blade to touch the ice, while defensemen who rely on maintaining position typically like more of the blade on the ice.

For young players, I recommend buying skates that fit. On the other hand, if you buy a pair a little big and have to grow into them, a couple of extra pairs of socks should help them fit. I realize that equipment can be expensive. But the proper equipment will help a player's performance and confidence. Skates are the most important piece of equipment for a hockey player. Buy the best you can afford.

Sticks

If you don't shoot, you don't score. And if you don't have a good stick, your chances of getting off a good shot fall. Sticks come in many shapes and materials. The traditional stick is made of wood. Some players, especially goaltenders, use all-wooden sticks, but modern players like a variety of materials including titanium, aluminum, fiberglass, kevlar, and graphite.

Blades are typically curved—either for a left-handed shot or a right-handed shot. A player with a right-handed shot holds his or her right hand lower on the stick. A player with a left-handed shot holds the left hand lower on the stick. The curve of the blade, along with a well-controlled snap of the wrists, can make for devastating accuracy.

Sticks are curved to give a player more control for shots from his or her normal shooting side.

In the NHL, sticks cannot measure longer than 63 inches from the heel to the end of the shaft. The blade length cannot measure more than 12½ inches. The blade must be between two and three inches wide, and the curve of the blade cannot be more than one-half inch. Sticks also have different degrees of flex—a measure of stiffness. Some players like an extra stiff stick to hit hard slap shots, while other players in close to the net like a little more flexibility in order to snap shots with precision.

Pads

Remember, hockey hurts. And to help prevent some of that hurting, players wear protective equipment. It doesn't eliminate the hurting, but it sure helps. Along with grace and athleticism, hockey is a game designed around smashing bodies and flying pucks. Thus, there are pads.

A hockey player wears a lot of equipment in order to keep safe.

It is simple physiology, the knee pad is connected to the knee, the shoulder pad is connected to the shoulder. The chest protector is in front of the chest, the helmet is on the head, a protective cup is around the groin, and the elbow pad protects the elbow. Shin guards protect the shins and gloves protect the hands. In addition, players wear a heavily padded girdle under their uniforms with pads protecting the hip, thigh, kidneys, and tailbone.

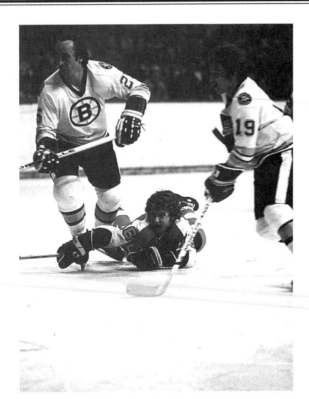

Equipment has improved from years ago when no one wore helmets and sticks were straight.

Protection has evolved quite a bit over the years. One piece of lore is that players used to use rolled-up newspapers or magazines stuffed inside their pant legs as shin pads. And, as you can tell by looking at old photographs, hockey players never used to wear helmets.

Despite all of this equipment, protection is not perfect. There are creases between pads, and sometimes players get hit in those areas. And the pads are not perfect either. A hit is a hit, and you feel it.

Goaltenders' Equipment— Once Again, Different

In the old days, goalies didn't wear masks. They had some pads and they held a big stick and a glove. And then they just stood there, waiting for the puck to fly in their direction. If it happened to hit them in the face, that was part of the job.

Equipment for goalies has improved since the early days of hockey when flesh and blood were considered pads.

In the book, *SAVE! Hockey's Brave Goalies* by Hal Bock (Avon, 1974), there is a short story about Hall of Fame goalie Chuck Rayner. Rayner, who played for the New York Rangers from 1940 to 1953, played without fear. Bock wrote, "Once, Chuck Rayner stopped a shot with his jaw and the save cost him four teeth. He underwent oral surgery to remove the roots of the broken teeth and was back in his cage the next night. He turned the other cheek, blocked another shot, and opened another gash in his already well-sutured profile. As he waited for the doctor to do some more hem-stitching, Rayner had this philosophical observation: 'It's a wonder,' he said, 'that somebody doesn't get badly hurt in this job.'" (Read more on the evolution of goalie masks in Chapter 7.)

Nowadays goalies wear masks and pads and still get to hold a big stick and a glove. The equipment for goalies is similar to the equipment for other players, yet different. For instance, although goalie skates look like the skates other players wear, goalies always have the entire blade on the ice for stability. The blade is usually longer than a regular skate blade, giving added stability. The boot itself is padded, as goalies often make stops with their boots.

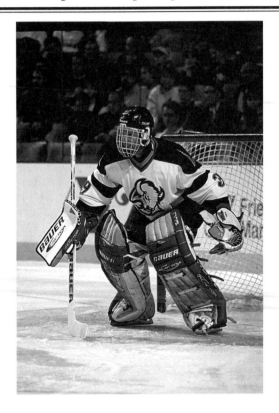

It's a dangerous job, therefore goalies wear a lot of equipment.

Sticks, too, are different—bigger, in order to deflect shots away from the goal. The blade can be longer than a regular stick, but no more than 15 1/2 inches in length. The blade cannot be wider than 3 1/2 inches. Above the blade of the hockey stick is a widened area that cannot be longer than 26 inches.

The hand that holds the stick wears a glove called a blocker, which has a flat rectangular back that can be used to block shots. The other hand wears a catching glove, which is a long glove that looks a lot like a first baseman's mitt in baseball. The pocket is deep and it allows a goalie to catch what goes in there.

Goalie pads are also bigger, mostly for protection, although some of the pads are bigger just to give the goaltender an extra few inches of edge in the battle to protect the goal.

Finally, the most important pieces of equipment are the mask and helmet. Helmets have only recently become popular in the NHL, and masks have only been popular for a few decades. As part of the mask, there is a throat protector, a sort of deflector pad hanging from the bottom of the mask. Safety, above all, is the purpose of all this equipment.

Extra Equipment Is Not an Excuse to Break Rules

Some players wear a plastic visor over their eyes. In youth leagues and college hockey, a visor or grid-pattern face shield is required. But not in the NHL. Many players who come into the NHL after years of wearing a face shield seem to naturally carry their stick higher than they should. This can and does cause a lot of facial injuries.

Players wearing masks should be aware that not everyone is wearing masks, and they should not let their sense of security influence where they hit another player. About 85 to 90 percent of pros don't wear a face shield. Yet, when a college player comes into the league, he often continues to wear a face shield because he is used to it. Often, he carries his stick high because he never used to worry about injuring another player's face. Equipment is worn as protection. It is not a license to illegally hit another player.

 ## *OFFSIDES*

The lines on the ice are not decorative. The Red Line and the two Blue Lines are on the ice to prevent a team, or players, from moving forward or ahead of the play too fast (too far in front of the puck carrier).

Essentially, offsides is called in two cases:

1. If there is a two-line pass. If the puck is behind the defensive Blue Line and is passed over the Blue Line and the Red Line, it is offsides. And if

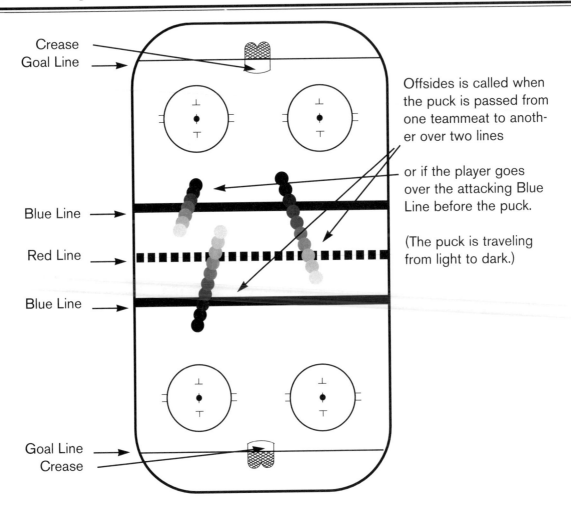

Crease
Goal Line

Offsides is called when the puck is passed from one teammeat to another over two lines

or if the player goes over the attacking Blue Line before the puck.

Blue Line

Red Line

(The puck is traveling from light to dark.)

Blue Line

Goal Line
Crease

the puck is behind the Red Line and is passed over the Red Line and the attacking Blue Line, it is offsides.

2. If an offensive player goes over the attacking Blue Line before the puck, offsides is called. The player's skates are what determine the judgment. Both skates have to be completely over the line for offsides to be called.

When an offsides occurs, the play is whistled dead and there is a face-off. In the first case, the face-off will be at the face-off point closest to the origination of the pass. In the second case, the face-off will occur at one of the face-off dots just outside the Blue Line.

 ## *ICING*

The rules of hockey do not allow the puck to fly back and forth across the ice without anyone touching it. The rules encourage skills. Thus, the rule of icing. This rule does not allow a defensive team to send the puck the full length of the ice without another player touching the puck.

The exception to this rule occurs when the defensive team is on the wrong side of a power play; in other words, when there are more offensive players on the ice than defensive players, due to a penalty. In that case, icing is allowed.

Icing is called when a player is behind the Red Line (also called Center Ice) and sends the puck all the way into the offensive zone (beyond the goal line) and the first person to touch the puck is a player on the other team who is not the goalie. As soon as a player on the defending team (who is not the goalie) touches the puck, play is stopped. If the goalie touches the puck or

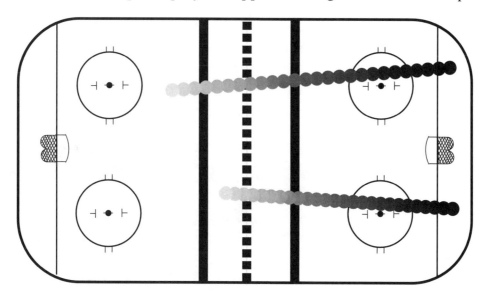

The puck crosses two or three lines and has to cross the goal line without going through the crease for icing to be called. The team whose end the puck is shot into has to touch the puck first or else the linesman will wave off the icing. Also, if a player doesn't make an honest effort to catch up to the puck before it crosses the goal line, it is usually waved off, at the discretion of the linesman.

if the puck goes through the crease, the icing is waved off. The linesman is the one who waves off an icing. When icing is called, the puck is brought all the way back to the defensive zone of the team that iced it. Thus, icing is only a temporary reprieve from the attacking team.

THOSE NASTY PENALTIES

Hockey is a contact sport and stuff happens; sometimes it's not always good. Then the referees have to step in and restore order. Almost always, the judgment of the referee rules. When punishment is needed, it usually comes in the form of banning a player from the ice for a certain number of minutes. There are three types of penalties: minor penalties, major penalties, and misconduct.

If you get a penalty, you are sent to the penalty box, a sort of short-term jail for hockey offenders. In most penalties (most penalties are minor penalties), the player in the box is not replaced on the ice. His or her team must play with one less player, unless a player from the other team is sent to the box (there is a wall dividing the penalty box). If you are in the box alone, leaving your team short-handed, you desperately want your team to stop the other team from scoring; it's a helpless feeling. If you get a penalty and the other team scores on a power play, it's a very lonely skate from the penalty box to the bench. You know that everyone is staring at you and at the scoreboard.

MINOR PENALTIES

Two-minute penalties. That's the most important thing to remember about minor penalties—the cost is two minutes off the ice in the penalty box.

Most penalties are minor penalties resulting from actions that are not intended to hurt. Here are a few examples.

Holding

If a player is caught holding his opponent or his opponent's stick, it is holding.

Holding onto a player or a player's stick is illegal.

Roughing

Like all penalties, this is called at the discretion of the referee. If the referee thinks a hit is intentionally made to hurt another player, he can call a major penalty. If two players simply get into a tiff with a lot of pushing and shoving but no one drops the gloves or intends to get into a fight, the penalty is simply roughing.

Tripping

This is often a last-chance attempt to stop an opponent from skating past a player and getting a better scoring advantage. Players sometimes also trip out of frustration at getting beat

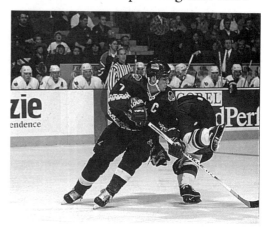

Tripping is illegal and dangerous.

down the ice. The referee must decide whether the tripping was intentional or incidental (and therefore legal), or an attempt by the offensive player to fake a penalty to get the defensive player into the penalty box.

Hooking

Just as vaudeville performers used to be pulled from the stage with a hooked cane, a player who is skating in for a goal can be hooked with a hockey stick—making forward progress difficult.

Interference

During a game, players are often fighting for position in front of the net, where this penalty is usually called. This penalty is called for interfering with the progress of a player who does not have the puck.

Hooking with the stick impedes the progress of a player and is therefore illegal.

It can be called for stopping a player who does not have the puck from moving, or it can even be called for stopping a player who has lost his stick from picking it up.

Slashing

If a player swings his stick at another player, even if contact is not made, it is slashing. This can be a minor, major, or misconduct penalty—depending on the discretion of the referee. Non-aggressive stick contact to the front of a player's shin pad is not penalized.

High-Sticking

If a player is carrying his stick above shoulder level when approaching another player, it is considered high-sticking. This rule is in place to protect the head and eyes.

Crosschecking

If both hands are on the stick but the stick is not on the ice, a player can be charged with a crosscheck if he hits an opponent with his stick.

Elbowing

It is not legal to use an elbow to hit an opponent.

Charging

If a player deliberately runs into another player after three strides or more with full force, he is usually called for charging. This can be a major penalty, depending on the discretion of the referee or the severity of the hit.

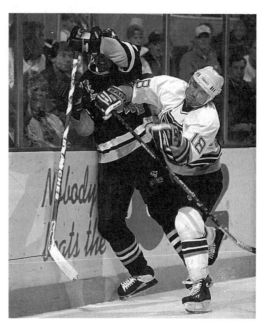

Using an elbow to check is illegal.

 # MAJOR PENALTIES

These penalties are given for bad behavior—the kind of stuff that appears to have the potential for injury. Referees don't look lightly on this behavior and the penalty reflects it. The penalty is five minutes. If an opposing player is injured in the face or head with a stick, the offending player is fined $100. Any player who receives three major penalties in one game is automatically thrown out, and a substitute will only be allowed in after five minutes.

Spearing

Stabbing an opponent with your stick is called spearing.

Fighting

Okay, here we go...let's talk about fighting. In some ways, it is part of hockey—always has been and always will be. At the same time, there is no room in hockey for fighting. So, what do I mean by this apparent contradiction?

Fighting is illegal. And yet the referees will let players go at it, at least for a little while. Referees are smart. They know what they are dealing with when they are around

Jabbing the stick into an opponent is dangerous and illegal.

NHL players and they aren't going to get in the middle of a tussle at the very beginning. First, they let the players who are fighting get tired—let them throw a few punches. Only then will the referees step in and take some action to break it up.

Don't get me wrong. Fighting is illegal, but it is also part of the game and it has been forever. The worst that can happen is a broken nose or hand. Emotions are flying high at the time and sometimes it is best to let the emotions run dry. Sometimes fighting can prevent injuries because it allows players to vent their frustrations and anger without smashing sticks or causing serious injury. The endgame of it all, though, is that fighting will bring a five-minute penalty.

Misconduct

Sometimes players really misbehave and this is when referees call a misconduct. There are three kinds of misconduct:

1. Misconduct is called for dangerous and intentional rule violations. The penalty is 10 minutes, but the team does not have to play short-handed. Instead, the player guilty of misconduct goes in the penalty box and is replaced on the ice by a teammate.

2. Game Misconduct is called when a player continually causes trouble (such as picking fights), or when he commits a particularly violent act. The player is immediately removed from the game, fined $200, and may face a league fine or suspension. A replacement player is immediately allowed on the ice. If a player receives three game misconducts in a season, he will automatically be suspended for a game.

Most of the time, fighting gives a psychological edge to the team that wins the fight. If your teammate is involved in a fight and wins, the entire team can gain energy. At the same time, if your teammate loses a fight badly, the reverse effect can occur. Depending on the situation of the game—taking into consideration the time in the game and the score—a fight may or may not have an impact on a team's psyche. Remember, hockey is a very physical sport and fighting epitomizes that aspecof itt.

3. Gross Misconduct is a referee's call and is considered even worse than a Game Misconduct. The player is immediately removed from the game and fined $200. A replacement player is immediately allowed on the ice. The case is referred to the League office for a possible fine or suspension.

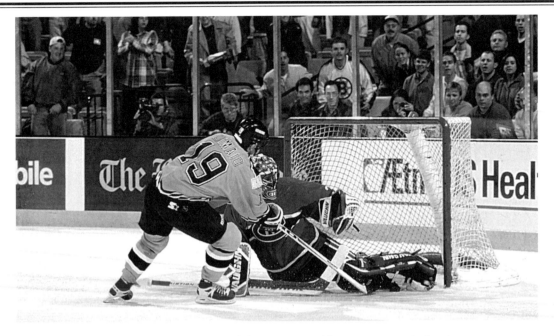

A penalty shot, though rare, is one of the most exciting moments in hockey.

 ## PENALTY SHOTS

Sometimes the referee will award a penalty shot. A player may be on his way alone toward the goalie and is tackled or tripped. In this instance, this call is up to the referee. If a player is going in on a breakaway and an opponent throws a stick, a penalty shot is automatically awarded. And if any defensive player in the crease (other than the goalie) covers the puck with his hands, a penalty shot is awarded. A penalty shot is pure excitement.

Everyone clears the ice except for a goalie and a skater from the opposing team. The puck is placed at center ice and the skater is given one chance to skate in on the goalie and shoot the puck. One on one. The skater must continue to move in a forward direction—as fast or as slow as he or she wants. If the player stops and goes backward, the shot is canceled.

The Players and the Strategies

Hockey flows. It is a game that has clearly defined positions on the ice, yet part of each position is ambiguous. Like melting ice, hockey positions blend into one another from time to time. Defensemen and forwards play different positions, and those positions are split even further—according to player type. There are many types of hockey players.

And then there are goalies.

There are specialty teams too that come on the ice for power plays. Hockey is a complex game and the player positions and strategies are also complex.

In this part, you will learn about the different positions and the various types of players and styles for each position. I will also mention some of the best players in the NHL in each of these positions. You will learn about goaltending and techniques, and you will learn some of the basic NHL strategies in today's game. There are many ways to try and score and to prevent being scored upon. You will learn some of the basics and see how they evolved.

4

Forwards

A**ny player on the ice is allowed** to score goals. Players with the specific job of scoring goals are called forwards: They play forward toward the other team's goal rather than back defending their own goal. In simplest terms, their job is to attack. However, it really isn't that simple because forwards also play back, often defending their own goal.

Wait a minute. Didn't he just say that forwards play forward, not back defending their own goal? Yes, I did. But that was in the simplest terms. The reality is that hockey is a very fluid game and roles are not strictly defined as in other sports. Forwards do have a defined role, but they are not confined by the definition. In fact, they had better be multi-dimensional or else the team will be in a lot of trouble when the opponents have the puck.

A CENTER AND TWO WINGS

There are actually three forwards on the ice: one center and two wings. The center plays in the center and the wings play on either side of the center. One is a left wing (who normally plays on the left side of the center) and the other is a right wing (who normally plays on the right side of the center). When the other team has the puck, forwards play a key role in the defense and their jobs are clearly defined. On offense, things are much more freewheeling, allowing forwards to utilize their skills across the ice in an effort to simply get the puck in the net.

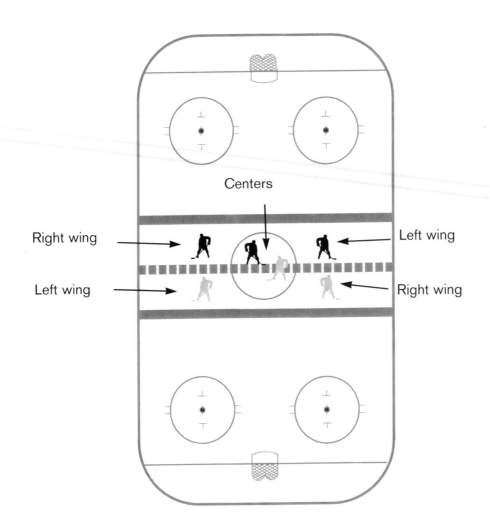

It's all a matter of perspective. This illustration shows the forwards on each team in their starting positions. A left wing on one team generally plays on the same side of the ice as the right wing on the other team. Left and right are decided by looking at the attacking goal.

FORWARDS ON DEFENSE, GET BACK!

No matter where the puck is on the ice, if one team has it, the other team is playing defense. Although forwards are expected to pressure the opposing team and score goals, they also play a lot of defense.

Forwards play defense mostly on the other team's defensemen. It works like this: If one team is advancing the puck and then there is a turnover, the forwards must immediately get back—fast. It's more like, *get back!* The idea is to never get beat down the ice by a defenseman. If a rushing defenseman beats a forward down the ice, it creates a mismatch—an odd-man rush, that is, two on one or three on two. Mismatches cause trouble.

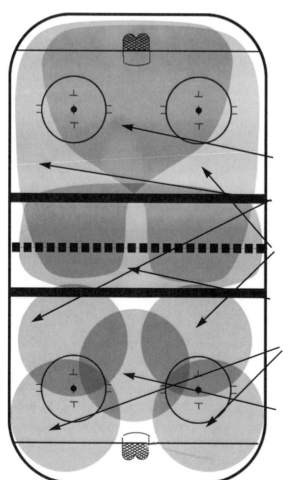

These are the general areas players cover. When there is a turnover, forwards have to immediately get back to their defensive position. If a wing gets back first, he goes to the middle and the center covers his side.

Center covers this area offensively.

Left wings cover this area on offense and defense.

Right wings cover this area on offense and defense.

Center ice players are usually given the green light offense in this area.

Left defense and right defense cover the front of the net.

Center plays a defensive role in this area.

Changing from offense to defense is absolute and instantaneous. The change back is just as absolute and instantaneous. But if a forward is in the attacking zone and suddenly there is a turnover, that forward has to get back and cover his zone on defense. Generally, forwards go to their specific zone, except that the first forward back always covers the middle. If a wing gets back first, the center then covers the wing's side.

When forwards are in their defensive positions, their primary job is to prevent defensemen from getting past them. They use body position to block defensemen from getting a free line at the goal. Forwards are tenacious in getting in the face of opponents quickly and not giving them any kind of room to make a play. While always thinking about making a break on offense, forwards are continually aware of the position of the defense and who has the advantage to get past.

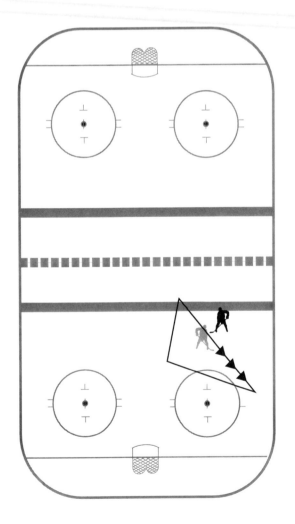

A forward uses body position to cut off angles for defensemen who want to rush the goal. A forward's position depends on the position of the defensemen.

FORWARDS ON OFFENSE, CHARGE!

When his team takes possession of the puck, a forward attacks, always aware, of course, of the rule of offsides. As soon as the turnover occurs, he busts out of the defensive zone. And once he is past his Blue Line, he has some freedom to move to different parts of the ice. Offense is a matter of creativity—a collaborative freelance operation of the three forwards and maybe a defenseman. There are no set plays, just a nod, a bob, a wave. Break! Break! Break! You don't yell it, you just think it. It's instinct and reaction.

The tough part comes when there is a turnover again because carte blanche on offense can produce some serious scrambling on defense. If you are on the wrong side of the ice when there is a turnover, you had better bust your body extra hard to get back.

Center

The center plays in the middle and takes the majority of face-offs. A player needs especially quick hands and fast reactions to win a face-off.

On defense, the center plays in front of the net and then moves into either corner if a defenseman needs help. Usually, a center moves into the corner if the puck is in there and the defenseman is up against more than one opposing player.

On offense, the center is free to create. Wings play off of the actions of the center, and vice versa. But overall, the center controls the play. If he heads to the left side, the left wing will cut to the center, and then reactions all follow from there.

Wings

Wings generally play on either side of the center in a role similar to the center. A right wing generally is on the right side (facing the defending goal) and shoots right-handed. A left wing generally plays on the left side and shoots left-handed. However, nothing is absolute and sometimes players play off-wing, meaning a left-handed shooter plays on the right side or a right-handed player plays on the left side.

On defense, wings cover their side of the ice unless they get back first. If a wing gets back first, he plays in front of the net, and the center plays on the wing. When there is a quick break or when the puck is sent down ice, the two players will quickly switch places. They switch when they can and when it doesn't create a disadvantage. On defense, wings are most concerned with the opposing defensemen getting past them.

On offense, wings play a variety of styles and roles. Ideally wings work well together and with the center to create opportunities to ultimately score goals. When one player charges the net, he brings a defenseman with him to open things up. Hockey is all about reactions and on offense, wings play offense. While on offense, however, some wings play a bit of defense. There are many styles of players and ultimately they all fit together into a team.

Power Forwards

A power forward takes position and doesn't relinquish it. When the opportunity arises, he is someone who plays physical. In the NHL, he will probably get in a fight from time to time because he won't back down from anyone. But a power forward is more than just physical. A power forward will score 40 to 50 goals a season.

A power forward prefers to have freedom to maintain position and not play against someone who is tough and physical. Usually, though, a power forward will face tough physical defenders. Most coaches like the matchup of strength against strength, but some defenders are simply annoying, like gnats. They are in your face, all around you. The space may be easier to maintain for the power forward, but the position of the defender can keep him off-balance.

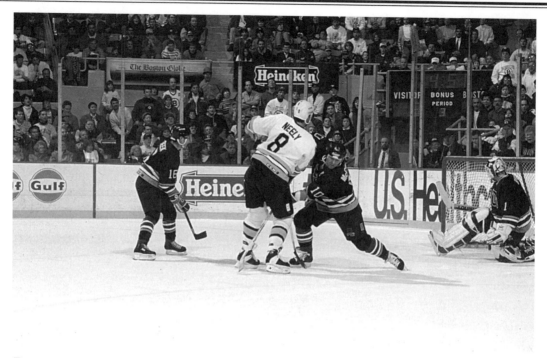

Power forwards are strong and physical and pay the price to maintain position.

Finesse Forwards

A finesse forward is a player who relies on skating and stickhandling ability to create opportunities. He can handle the puck well, has a lot of moves, can beat people with speed, and can score 30, 40, or 50 goals a season. This forward's skill is more speed and finesse than strength. A finesse forward won't physically intimidate anyone but can sometimes fake an opponent out of his or her skates. This is considered a form of intimidation.

Finesse works well for centers, who rely on their ability to move and fake people out. It can also work well for some wings, as long as at least one of the wings is a physical player. You cannot have too much power and strength, but you can keep opposing teams off-balance by mixing in some finesse.

MIXING AND MATCHING

Different forwards have different levels and types of skills. A forward who is offensive-minded can handle the puck really well and can score. A forward who is more defensive-minded may not necessarily score a lot of goals but he can go on the ice for a shift and shut the other team down. These types of players are often used against the other team's top offensive players. However, I prefer to match offense against offense. Mixing and matching skills and lines in hockey is a matter of personal preference for the coach.

All coaches want to have at least some strength and intimidating power on the ice to protect their finesse players. But power players provide more than protection. They allow for opportunity. Hockey is a mental game about speed and power and turf (in hockey, of course, the turf is ice). Power helps protect some of the ice.

Teams often have a first line, a second line, and a third line that rotate in throughout the game. Coaches prefer to stay with set lines, although often they don't. Again it all depends on the coach's intuition and whether the coach thinks things are working. Coaches are paid to make decisions that work. They make decisions, and some of them work. That's hockey coaching.

The Enforcer

An enforcer is generally a forward who goes anywhere on the ice to create deliberate havoc. If anything happens—a dirty check, a run at a star—the tough guy from down the end of the bench will come into the game to even the score. He'll try to calm things down by starting a fight or creating an altercation of some kind.

There are teams that have more than one player known more for fighting than for hockey skills. It is better now than it was 15 or 20 years ago when there were players who weren't even good hockey players. Now, at least, the enforcers can play hockey too. And there is an average of about two enforcers per team.

Enforcers are always out there to send a message. Sometimes at the end of a blow-out game—say the score is 5 to 1 with not much time left—a coach will send his so-called tough guys out to create something. A little something, just to make sure the other team remembers that when they play again, it won't be a walk in the park.

Breakouts

When a team recovers the puck in its own zone, it needs to break out into the attacking zone. There is a standard breakout that works because of the options it gives to the team with the puck. The breakout works in a mirrored way, depending on the side of the ice where the puck is when the team starts forward.

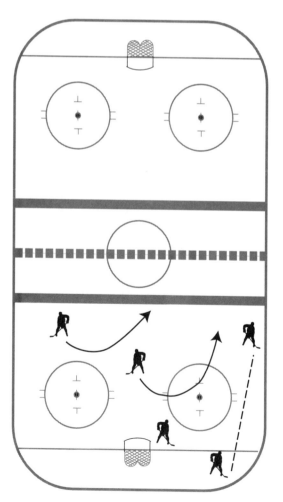

If the puck is coming down the right side, the center is going to go near the puck to create a 2-on-1 situation. And then, the left wing will move toward the center of the ice to create an easier passing lane. There are three options for the right wing with the puck: Keep it, pass it to the center, or pass it to the left wing. In the freewheeling nature of hockey, there are a million options for each player. But the basics of a right-side breakout look like this illustration.

A right-side breakout gives the right wing three options to advance the puck up the ice.

Once the puck is into the attacking zone, one player will rush the goal, bringing a defender or two to create open space.

Smart Plays

Things don't always work the way you hope. That's when forwards are expected to play smart hockey and make smart decisions. For instance, if a forward is moving the puck forward but does not have a lane to skate the puck through, he may instead dump it into the attacking zone. But if he dumps it near the goalie, who can then shovel it to a defenseman, it is just like giving the other team the puck. Instead, the idea is to dump the puck to an area where the other team has to turn around to chase it, and the odds are close to even that you or your teammate can get there first. That's smart hockey.

 ## SHOTS

All players, including defensemen, can shoot the puck. Forwards generally do the most shooting and they have a variety of shots at their disposal.

Slap Shot

A slap shot requires a big windup and the puck can travel faster than 100 miles per hour. As the slap shot takes time to get the shot away (because the backswing is higher than other shots), a player usually needs to be in open space in order to take one that won't get blocked or deflected.

The best time for a player to take a slap shot is when he or she is moving toward the goal and has time to take the shot but cannot get any closer. Despite the fact that a slap shot can travel so fast, goalies stop most slap shots. When a good goalie sees the puck, the goalie usually can stop it. The key to making the slap shot is to get a good angle and pick a corner that will get the goalie off-balance.

Snap Shot

There is virtually no backswing on a snap shot. It is all wrist, a quick little snap sending the puck flying in a precise direction. This shot is not as fast as a slap shot, so it is usually shot in closer to the net. But a snap shot can be deadly accurate.

Backhand

Even though hockey sticks are curved to shoot with the forehand, all players are very accurate shooting a backhand. The puck simply comes off the back of the stick with a flick of the wrists. Although the backhand shot is not used often, it should still be worked on in practice. Although the backhand does not necessarily travel at great speeds, it is a difficult shot for a goalie to stop because it can be disguised. Just ask any goalie.

 ## PLANNING TO GET A BREAK

Often, scoring is a matter of being in the right place at the right time with the right set of reactions. You have to read the play from where the shot is going to where the rebound might go. You should also try to get to know the goalie's strengths and weaknesses. That can mean understanding that the goalie is not just in the way of the target but realizing that he can also be used to bounce the puck off of to get it in the goal. Bouncing the puck off the back of the goalie's leg and getting it in is great fun.

Bing Bing Bing

Sometimes the puck will bounce from stick to stick in rapid-fire fashion. The whole thing happens in a matter of one second and the first pass sets up the sequence. By the time the puck hits the third stick, it is a matter of redirecting the shot. There is no swing at all, simply a well-placed stick.

The Spectacular Skating Shot

There is magic and deceit on the ice and sometimes a great player can use both to score a goal that leaves players out of position and lurching in the wrong direction. Often, a shot doesn't stand on its own but is the result of a number of actions. In this case, it comes as the result of the spectacular actions of one player zooming and weaving down the ice.

 ## *MY TOP 10 FORWARDS*

I began playing in the NHL in 1983 and have seen many great players. Here is a list, in no special order, of the 10 best forwards I have seen play since 1983.

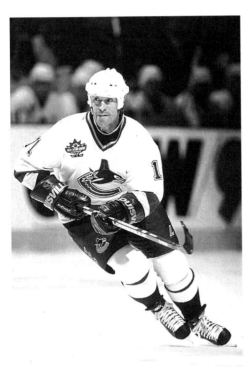

Mark Messier Center with Edmonton, New York Rangers, and Vancouver. This guy has won six Stanley Cups. He is a physical player with a great gift for offense and is a fiery team leader.

Wayne Gretzky Center with Edmonton, Los Angeles, St. Louis, and the New York Rangers. Probably the best hockey player who ever lived, the ultimate playmaker. Gretzky possesses great vision and is able to anticipate the flow of the game with a press-box perspective.

Mike Bossy A right wing with the New York Islanders, retired in 1987. He won four Stanley Cups and was a finesse player and a great scorer with perhaps the fastest release ever. Bossy was a phenomenal scorer, able to shoot before the goalie was ready.

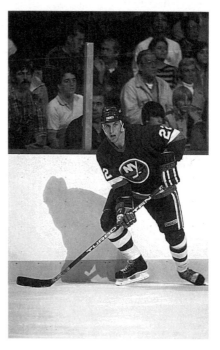

Clark Gillies Left wing with the New York Islanders team that won four Stanley Cups, retired in 1988. He was a tough hockey player who was a physical presence on the ice. Gillies was an imposing force, unafraid to drop the gloves and fight, but more than able to score goals.

Ron Francis A center who started with Hartford and is now in Pittsburgh. He didn't get the recognition he deserved in Hartford (due to lack of media). When he went to Pittsburgh, he was another player in Mario Lemieux's shadow. He quietly goes about his business putting numbers on the board year after year. Francis is not only great offensively but is one of the best defensive centers in the league as well.

◀ ***Mario Lemieux*** Center with the Pittsburgh Penguins who retired in 1997. He won two Stanley Cups and was a perfect package of size and skills. Although he wasn't a physical player, he did have the size to ensure he wouldn't get pushed around. Lemieus was a superb skater and stickhandler.

◀ **Steve Yzerman** Center who won the 1997 Stanley Cup with the Detroit Red Wings. He plays bigger than he is. Although he is not a large player, he plays with authority on the ice. Yzerman gets into the mix and gets his nose dirty.

Brendan Shanahan Right wing who played for New Jersey, St. Louis, Hartford, and is currently with the Detroit Red Wings. Shanahan is a power forward who is physical, can score goals, and set up plays.

Eric Lindros A big imposing center with Philadelphia. He has the total package of skills—a physically imposing great skater who can shoot and set up plays.

Adam Oates My teammate with the Bruins who is now with Washington. The best playmaker I ever played with, Oates was great on face-offs and in the corners.

FIVE FORWARDS I CAN'T LEAVE OUT

The following forwards are also exceptional:

Jaromir Jagr Right wing with the Penguins, who won two Stanley Cups. He was in Mario Lemeiux's shadow, but people are now beginning to understand just how good Jagr is. He is a powerful skater with a great shot and a creative playmaker who is very strong on his feet.

Peter Forsberg Center with Colorado is another player with playmaking and scoring abilities. Forsberg is a solid two-way hockey player.

Paul Kariya Center with Anaheim is phenomenal. There has been talk in Paul's young career that he sees the ice almost like Wayne Gretzky at his prime. He is a fantastic playmaker who can score as well.

Teemu Selanne Right wing with Anaheim has great outside speed with a fantastic shot. He is always dangerous with the puck.

◄ **Keith Tkachuk** Left wing who I consider a great power forward with the Phoenix Coyotes. Tkachuk is a very physical player who can score 40 to 50 goals a year.

Defensemen

Each team has two defensemen, left and right, and they generally have the same job description. They cover the front of the net and the defensive corners and, as part of covering in front of the net, they try and clear out rebounds from the goalie before the offense on the opposing team can get to them. The goal of a defenseman is to prevent goals.

But defensemen play more than defense. That's right, just like forwards, defensemen are hockey players and hockey players play hockey. For defensemen, this means that sometimes they will attack with the offense. But, most important of all, defensemen protect the goal.

DEFENSE EQUALS POSITION

The aim of defense is to cut off angles to the net. Defensemen are doing a good job when they make their goalie's job easier. Usually, the two defensemen will not play extremely close together but will instead work together to cut off angles to the net and protect the corners.

Defensemen primarily cover in front of the crease and the defensive corners.

When the puck goes into a defensive corner, one defenseman goes in after it and the other one "stays home" in front of the net, cutting off angles from that side. If the puck goes into the defensive left corner (remember, left and right are determined by which goal you call the attacking goal), the left defenseman will go in after it (along with the center) and the right defenseman will cover in front of the goal. If it goes into the right corner, the defensemen shift roles.

If the puck goes around the back of the net, the defensemen still shift roles. Covering in front of the net always takes priority. At least one defenseman should always stay home, shifting with the movement of the puck while making sure no opposing player gets open in front of the net.

Hit 'Em Hard

Defensemen are usually big and they always like to hit hard to make sure that offensive players know they are around. They want position and more. Defensemen want offensive players to know there is a price for going in front of the net. That price is usually a series of solid body checks. Often, muscle and the ability to take a hit are key components of hockey players on both offense and defense. But offensive players (at least some) can get away with being finesse players. Defensemen need to be able to hit.

Body checks work to disrupt the puck carrier or to disrupt the progress of a skater. A really good check will leave your opponent sprawled on the ice. Checks can be made with the full body, the shoulder, or the hip. A *body check* calls for the defenseman to push his full body against the other player. In a *shoulder check*, the defenseman thrusts one shoulder into the chest of the opponent. In a *hip check*, the defenseman bends over slightly and uses his hip to bang into the other player.

The Best Defense Is a Good Offense

A defenseman is often a key figure in a team's offense. That's right—offense. Not all NHL defensemen are great on offense, but those who can play offense bring an extra charge to any offense. Any offensive line would love to have them. When defensemen rush with the offense and charge the goal, there is greater opportunity for that team to outman the opposing team and create more scoring chances. But remember, defensemen must also be careful not to be caught out of position when there is a turnover. They should only rush when they feel confident of their chances. After all, the extra man up helps the numbers game.

When a defenseman attacks, the offense takes a risk that the extra man is worth the chance of an odd-man rush (one more offensive player in the attacking zone than there are defensive players) the other way. It can and does happen. If there is a sudden turnover, a defenseman in the attacking zone doesn't do a lot of good defending his goal.

When a defenseman rushes on offense, it gives the offense one extra player to pass to and to help the play.

Two Different Kinds

When a defenseman has the skills to attack, he is considered an offensive defenseman. When his skills are more confined to his specialty of defense, he is considered a defensive defenseman. For the most part, an offensive defenseman is usually paired up with a defensive defenseman.

A defensive defenseman will rarely go past the offensive Blue Line. On offense, this type of player will help move the puck forward. He will skate in behind the forwards but won't usually jump into the play. He is not going to charge the goal or look for inside rebounds. He is always concentrating on stopping anyone from beating him down the ice to his own goal and is always thinking about position and angles.

An offensive defenseman is also thinking about defense first, but he is not afraid to take risks from time to time. He will attack when he sees an opportunity and will often act as a leader of the offense. He will jump into the play over the offensive Blue Line to see if he can help make something good happen. Offensive defensemen can control the play and are great shooters. Most are big and when an offensive defenseman displays some finesse as well, it can be devastating to the opposing team. When an offensive defenseman sees an opening, he jumps into the play—skating through holes, looking for position, watching the play develop, and helping it along. An offensive defenseman who is attacking simply plies his art—he plays hockey, skating and stopping and constantly ready to skate back and defend the flag. He is an offensive defenseman, but first of all, he plays defense.

The Best Time to Play the Best Guy

Every team wants to have at least one great offensive defenseman, and then the strategy is to always pair that defenseman up with the best offensive line. The aim is to get the best offensive skills together on the ice and see what they can create. But some offensive lines are almost defensive in nature. It would not be as useful offensively if a great offensive defenseman was teamed with a line of forwards who did not have great offensive skills. Some lines are like cavalry. The best offensive defensemen belong with the power lines that attack and crave strength and creativity. Also, every team would like an offensive defenseman for the power play. Specialty teams are important in today's games.

 ## INTENTIONAL ICING: CLEARING THE PUCK

If the offensive team is just buzzing around getting a lot of scoring opportunities and the defensemen can't seem to get control, sometimes the best thing to do is to ice the puck. It's called clearing the puck, which is intentional icing. This is not necessarily the best strategy in many situations, but if the offense clearly has control and keeps getting rebounds and creating all-around havoc in front of the net, the defensemen sometimes need to regroup. The best way is to simply get a whack at the puck and send it down the ice to the other end.

That way you can calm the situation down and also get some fresh players on the ice. Even though the face-off comes back to your end, your team will get a break from the onslaught.

It is not a good strategy to do this if your team is controlling the puck. Icing is a mistake in that situation. But if your goalie is making great save after great save and your team can't control rebounds and breakdowns are turning into multitudes of opportunities for the opponent, icing is a good option.

SAFE PLAYS

When defensemen are back on defense, they don't take chances. When a defenseman takes possession of the puck in his own defensive zone, he does everything possible to keep it or to pass it safely to one of his teammates. A safe pass never crosses in front of the defending goal and is usually a short pass. It is direct and sure, a secure placement on the next player's stick.

This is not always possible, of course, but when the puck is in the defensive zone, or even behind the goal line, defensemen must be very careful about where it goes. The two best options, obviously, are to keep the puck and advance it or pass the puck to a teammate who can advance it. Those two opportunities, however, do not always present themselves. The next option is to put the puck in a safe place. Usually, defensemen will wrap it tight around the boards to let the wings handle it or they will try to chip it out of the zone.

Dumping It into a Safe Place—Using the Boards

A safe place is someplace on the ice that, even if the opponent does get to it first, he cannot easily turn it into a scoring opportunity. Always make 'em work for it.

One of the best ways for a defenseman to do this is to send the puck around the back of the boards, right past the other defenseman, and up the ice. The hope, of course, is that one of the forwards can catch up to it. When a forward catches up, a breakout can occur.

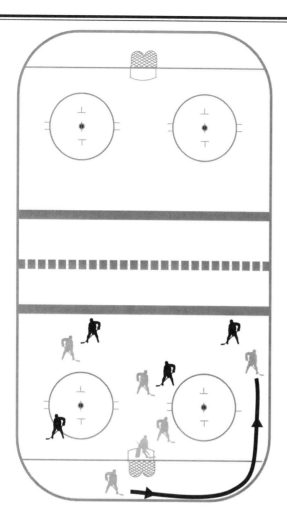

When the puck is passed around the boards behind the net, the defensive team has a chance for an offensive breakout, and it theoretically gives the forward with the puck some options to advance it. (Lighter colored players are in their defensive zone but have control of the puck.)

More realistically, the other team will recover and have to start over trying to set things up. Still, the defensive team will have time to regroup and maybe even bring in substitutions.

Using the back boards is an interesting concept, similar to using defensive territory for an offensive advantage. Of course, it starts as a defensive purpose. The boards, and not just the back boards, are often used as an extra player. Passes can be bounced off the boards, just as they can be sent around the back of the boards. Hockey players understand perfectly well that hockey pucks bounce off the walls.

As soon as the puck comes around the back of the net and heads up the ice along the side, the attacking team should then get the puck to the middle as it continues up the ice. Offense always wants the puck near the middle of the ice, while defense has a priority to clear the puck out of the middle.

Acting Like Goalies

There are some defensemen who like to act like goalies and block shots when deemed necessary. Some of these players are quite good and willing to throw their body in the way of the puck. These guys are not exactly frustrated goalies. After all, they don't play full-time goalie, but maybe they are smarter. They bring an extra defensive skill into the mix. Blocking shots is a superb skill that involves supreme timing, guts, and superior hand-eye coordination.

MY TOP 10 DEFENSEMEN

I began playing in the NHL in 1983 and I have seen many great players. Here is a list, in no special order, of the 10 best defensemen I have seen play since 1983:

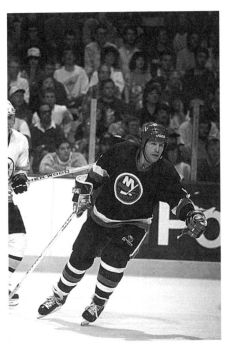

Denis Potvin Won four Stanley Cups with the New York Islanders. The Islanders built their team around this guy, who was great at both ends of the ice. A solid body checker, many considered Potvin the best defenseman of the early eighties.

Ray Bourque A teammate of mine with the Bruins who has done it all for years both offensively and defensively—a strong presence while he's on the ice.

Chris Chelios Plays with Chicago and is a great competitor. I had many battles with him when he was with Montreal. He is a defenseman you would love to have on your team.

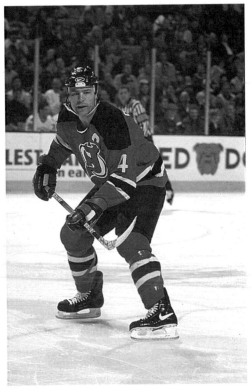

◀ **_Scott Stevens_** A big, strong, tough defenseman with New Jersey who plays the body extremely well and can really control his end of the ice and control you.

Larry Robinson A classic hall-of-famer who played with Montreal. I played against him at the end of his career. Robinson was so big and strong that it was hard to get an advantage on him.

Rob Blake A player with Los Angeles who doesn't get the recognition he deserves but is a solid two-way defenseman.

◀ **_Brian Leetch_** A great offensive defenseman with the New York Rangers. Leetch has also learned to play in the defensive zone, which makes him that much better. As a right winger you really have keep an eye on him in the offensive zone.

Kevin Lowe Now back with Edmonton, where he won five Stanley Cups, he also won a cup with the New York Rangers. Lowe is a very underrated defenseman. I had many battles against him. Lowe gets in your face and does what he needs to do to help the team win. He is relentless.

Craig Ludwig Played with Montreal and is now with Dallas. Another underrated player. A great defensive defenseman who doesn't give you much room. Ludwig is not afraid to give up his body to block shots. Check out his shinpads—they look like a small set of goalie pads.

Mark Tinordi Played with Minnesota and Dallas and is now with Washington. You may not notice him but if you are playing in a game against him, you know he is playing.

FIVE I CAN'T LEAVE OUT

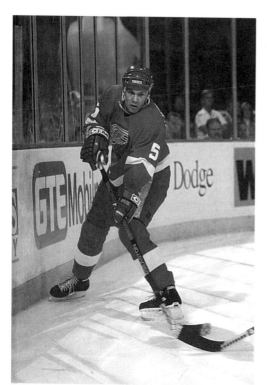

◀ ***Nicklas Lidstrom*** A great offensive defenseman with Detroit who has a long bright future ahead of him. He is one of the NHL's most gifted defensemen.

Bryan Berard Plays with the New York Islanders and has been compared at times to Brian Leetch. He is learning the game quickly at both ends of the ice.

Derian Hatcher Plays with Dallas and is a big, strong, tough defenseman who will not give you any room.

Sandis Ozolinsh A great offensive defenseman with Colorado. He is very dangerous, especially on the power play.

Ed Jovanovski A big, strong, tough defenseman for the Floridas Panthers who is still learning the game. I am looking for him to be a solid defenseman for years to come.

6

Specialty Teams

When there is a penalty and a player must serve time in the penalty box, one team will have a numbers advantage on the ice. This is a situation for specialty teams.

On offense, this is the power play, and the offense usually has its best chance to score. Numbers advantages are important: Power plays give the offense a rare opportunity to actually set something up rather than just freelance at a frantic pace.

On defense, there are penalty killers. The offense has the numbers advantage and the defense has to stop anything from happening in (usually) two minutes. Penalty killers come in hoping to kill off those two minutes without giving the opposing team a clear shot on goal. It is a difficult task playing with a teammate down, but it is done with angles, good goaltending, and sometimes luck.

STUFF HAPPENS

Hockey is hockey—a tough, action-oriented sport of strong-willed hockey players who sometimes do things that they are not supposed to do.

When that happens (and they are caught), they often have to serve time in the penalty box. (Penalties and their price are described in Chapter 3).

Players sometimes do illegal things, and often not on purpose. It is the nature of the sport. There are infractions in any sport. In hockey, infractions can sometimes be a bit more physical than infractions in, say, croquet. But hockey is a sport with rules, and rules are sometimes broken.

When a player gets beat, a natural reaction is to do anything to keep an opponent from getting some open ice in front of the goal. And anything can mean grabbing, holding, or hooking. An opponent skates by and you grab. It is not necessarily a conscious decision to stop him, although sometimes it is. You may think at the time that a penalty is better than letting a player have a free shot or what appears to look like an easy opportunity for a goal. Specialty teams play as the result of a penalty.

 ## SPECIAL PLAYS

Suddenly, there is an advantage and both teams quickly make changes to adjust. The team with the advantage, sensing opportunity, will most likely put its five best offensive players on the ice together. It doesn't matter if only one or even none of them is a defensemen. The chance is there to score and the team with a numbers advantage will put their best weapons together. But rarely will you see five forwards on a power play. A short-handed goal is something you don't want to give up.

If the best players were already on the ice at the beginning of a power play, a coach may take them off for a quick 30 seconds of rest and then leave them in for the last minute and a half of a two-minute power play. The team that is shorthanded will want its best defensive players on the ice. Their main goals are to hold position and play angles. And sometimes the best defensive players are also quite good offensively, so if they see an opportunity to score, they will go for it.

At the end of a power play, one team gets a tremendous lift. If the team on the power play scores, well, they score! Enough said. But if the other team stops them and kills the penalty, that team gets a huge boost, especially if it's a 5-on-3 power play. The psychology of a power play is that one team is guaranteed to come out of it happy and one team will be disappointed.

Power Plays on Offense

When a power play begins and the team at full strength has the puck, there is time to set up. The player with the puck has a little more time to carry it than normal because of the numbers advantage and the fact that the defense will stay back and not take as many chances. After all, if the defense goes for the puck and is beat, the numbers advantage is even worse. So the defense usually lays back.

Power Forwards on Power Plays

The offense will often try to get its best power forward in front of the net to serve two purposes:

1. Screen the goalie from seeing any shots. Another player guards the power forward, so that player screens the goalie too.
2. Get rebounds and tip-ins.

As always, the power forward will take abuse in this position in front of the net. When he gets there and tries to stay there, the defense will do what it can to make his life miserable. He gets crosschecks, banged on the back of the legs, anything and everything. And on the power play, the defense will get away with a little bit more, so the power forward has to basically grin and bear it, pay the price for the chance to score.

But a power forward can give the team a tremendous advantage if he is able to stay in there and serve those two roles. When he does that, the offense wants to shoot as soon as it can to get some action going in front

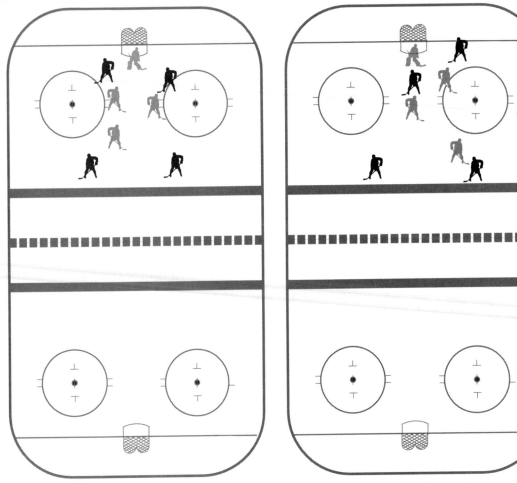

The penalty killers will be in a triangle. The forward will force the defense and try to take away passing lanes. Also, 1 defenseman will try to help out up top, depending which side the puck is on. There is a lot of rotating in this situation.

This is the hardest of all situations to be in, for obvious reasons. The best the penalty killers can do is try to get their sticks in passing lanes and force only when they are 100% sure of not getting beat.

of the net. The power forward will be involved in some set plays (the power play is the only time that there is an opportunity to try something like set plays in the flowing game of hockey). Generally, however, the power forward is playing a reaction game, waiting for the puck, working with teammates, and looking for holes to jump into. He wants to get away from defensemen for just a second in order to receive a pass and get a shot off quickly.

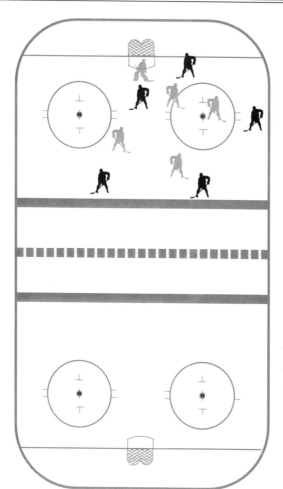

The penalty killers will be in a box. They will try to keep the puck on the perimeter and again keep their sticks in passing lanes.

The European Style

Many European players have been successful with a different strategy. Quite simply, they keep moving and weaving up the ice with a series of short passes and keep the passes going until somebody is open with a clear shot at the goal. Sometimes you will see these types of players looking for the pass that is going to set up an open net. But they may not find that open pass. By continuing to look for that pass, the team may lose a good chance to create other scoring opportunities.

Wayne Gretzky is a master at setting up the power play from behind the enemy net.

The Gretzky Way

Wayne Gretzky has spent his career revolutionizing the power play by setting things up from behind the net. He basically forces a defender to come get him. When the defender comes from one side, Gretzky goes to the other side and puts the defender out of position. And then he has an unbelievable ability to find the open man.

Wayne is also one of the first, if not the very first, player I have seen pass the puck off the net and back to himself or to other players.

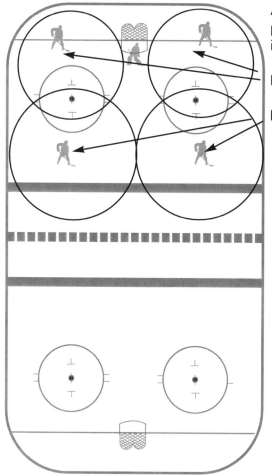

A typical 4-player defense against a power play creates a hopefully impenetrable box in front of the net.

Penalty Killing defense

Penalty Killing forward

DEFENSE: DRAWING THE BOX

A standard strategy with four strong players against a power play of five is to divide the defensive zone into four quadrants and assign each player to a quadrant. If a player is drawn out of his or her quadrant, you should see the players rotate to fill the gap and still maintain the box. The area does not extend throughout the entire defensive zone, but instead creates a sort of box that the four players try to own. If each defenseman can keep the puck out of his or her box, they will force the offense to take low percentage shots from the perimeter.

Forcing the Play

Some teams will play the four quadrants and then force the play in whichever quadrant the puck goes. In other words, as soon as the puck enters a quadrant, the player defending that quadrant will rush the puck handler, forcing him to make a play. If the defense is faster than the offense, this works because it doesn't give the offense time to think and set anything up. But if the defense isn't fast enough, the defense can get burned. If you hesitate, you are lost in no-man's land. You have to decide as soon as the puck enters your quadrant whether to force the play or not.

Some teams will even put two forwards up high and make it hard for a team to even bring the puck into the offensive zone. This is a risky philosophy when you are trying to kill a penalty, but some players are good enough to make it work.

Pull the Goalie

Things sometimes get desperate for hockey teams. Two sets of numbers—the score and the time remaining—lead to this feeling of desperation. When a hockey team is truly at a level of now-or-never, they will perform a desperate, but sometimes successful, act. The coach will decide to pull the goalie in order to give the team on offense a numbers advantage. Of course, this strategy relies on maintaining near constant control of the puck as there is an open net that is not being protected by a goalie. The only time this is done is late in a game when a team desperately needs a goal to get back into the game. Different coaches have different philosophies on when to pull the goalie. Most like to wait until there are fewer than two minutes remaining in the game. Some coaches wait even longer, with only one minute to 1:15 remaining. It's the coach's call. After all, a loss is a loss. Whether it is 3 to 2 or 4 to 2, it's still a loss. So teams sometimes try to even the score at the risk of losing by more.

Goalies

oalies are a different breed. Everyone who plays hockey and doesn't play goalie says the same thing about all goalies—different. Goalies may not be insane but they sure do act as if having a hard rubber object flying in their direction doesn't bother them. They act as if they like it. What possible explanation is there? Goalies are, well, different. Most are often proud to be wackier than the average person. As the great Gump Worsley, who played more than 20 years with the New York Rangers, Montreal Canadiens, and Minnesota North Stars, once said: "You don't have to be nuts to be a goalie, but it helps." Worsley, who played in the 1950s, 1960s, and 1970s, stated: "My face is my mask."

For a hockey team, a goalie is the most important player on the ice. A goalie can almost single-handedly win a game, or at least influence the outcome, more than any other player. When a goalie gets hot, he can carry the team by making spectacular saves, energizing the team, and simply stopping the other team from scoring. After all, zero never wins.

NO FEAR

It is impossible for pads to be flexible enough to work right and provide protection for every square inch of the body—there are little holes in the protection between the pads. It is not unusual to see goalies walking around with bruises on their shoulders, arms, and back of their legs. Besides games, goalies take hundreds of shots in practice every day. They can't worry about fear; they focus on stopping the puck. And it is certainly easier than it was in the old days when goalies didn't wear masks. Masks have evolved quite a bit from the 1970s when goalies like the Boston Bruins' Gerry Cheevers wore a form-fitting facemask. Cheevers' mask was unique because he decorated it with the markings of stitches. Nowadays goalies wear huge catchers-type helmets that are much more protective than the old kind.

In the 1970s, Gerry Cheevers, a premier goalie with the Boston Bruins, was known for his facemask of stitches (on right) and brilliant saves. Goalies nowadays wear a full mask.

STRATEGY: ALL THE ANGLES

Goalies play angles. For instance, if the puck is in the corner, the goalie knows that the shooter has a bad angle to try to get the puck in the net. If the puck moves toward the middle of the ice, the shooter has a better angle because he can get the puck into more of the net. Thus, there is more of the net for the goalie to cover. If there is one shooter coming down the ice, the goalie may come out of the net a little to force a faster decision and to make the angles tougher on the shooter. Of course, if the skater with the puck has other players to pass to, the goalie won't come out at all. The goalie always covers the player with the puck.

 ## HAND-EYE COORDINATION

The puck travels at high speeds. It gets deflected. It bounces and slides under legs or in the air, amidst fast and furious action—arms, sticks, and skates flying and colors, noise, and distracting thoughts. The goalie focuses, reacts, and then something happens.

 ## THE HOLES

When shooters shoot, they learn to shoot at the different holes as a way of gaining accuracy and identifying goals. Those holes are illustrated below.

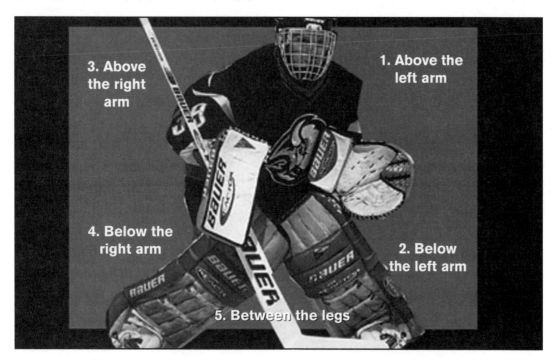

A number defines each hole in the goalie's standard stance.

GUTS AND GLORY—
OR THE GOALIE'S THE GOAT

Goalies are heroes. When they do their impossible job of stopping that little puck that players wearing the wrong color try with great vigor to get past them with fast shots, precision passes, lucky bounces, and slick chicanery, goalies make life for their teammates a lot easier. When they do not do the job of stopping the puck, well, goalies can be goats. That's what people say. Teams lose, and goalies lose. People do not usually refer to forwards or defensemen losing games, unless they manage to do it in a noticeable way. When goalies don't do their job, it is very noticeable.

GOALIE COMMUNICATION

Some goalies talk. There is often communication going on between the goalie and the defensemen. The goalie will tell the defense when they have time to get the puck or when they have to get rid of it in a hurry. The defense appreciate the help, as the goalie is seeing things that they don't.

HANDLING THE PUCK

If a goalie can skate well and handle the puck well, he is able to get to a dumped puck quicker and can make a more accurate pass to start a breakout. The other team is always aware when a goalie is a good skater. They will be careful not to dump the puck into an area where the goalie can get to it easily. When a goalie such as Ron Hextall comes out and handles the puck, the other team knows he creates a great opportunity for his team to get a quick breakout. At times, he can act like a third defenseman, quite an advantage for a team. If the opposing team dumps the puck in to allow time for a line change, a good stickhandling goalie can move the puck quickly to a teammate and create a breakaway. I know, I've seen it many times.

PSYCH GAMES

Hockey can be like a mental war (as well as a physical tiff) on the ice for all hockey players. The battle waged between the offense of one team and the goalie of another is a match of wits, reflexes, nerve, speed, position—the list is endless. At the end of it, on defense, the goalie at least appears to have the ultimate responsibility. The goalie, of course, is not the only one at fault if a shot goes in the net, but the goalie is the one everyone sees.

Every one of a goalie's actions—a great save, a cheap goal let in—sends a message. If he has stopped a great scorer from scoring on him for the past few games, maybe he just knows he has the scorer's number, and in this case, the scorer is not a scorer. When a goalie is on, he lays a perfect trap—*I dare you to score on me*. There is no logical explanation for it. (Sometimes great scorers get the number of a great goalie as well.) Goalies study shooters. As a shooter, I studied goalies. I knew their strengths and weaknesses, their different techniques and styles.

 ## BUTTERFLY GOALIES

Some goalies have a way of protecting the corners by sticking their arms and hands out and pushing their knees together to cover the middle while pushing their feet out to cover the bottom corners. The pose is that of a butterfly. In addition, there is the freelance flying aspect of the glove and stick moving in reaction to the shot. A goalie goes wherever the wind (and the puck) take him. Patrick Roy of the Colorado Avalanche is a great example of a butterfly goalie.

A butterfly goalie spreads his wings to go after the puck.

STAND-UP GUYS

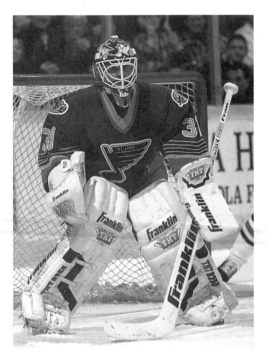

All goalies stand, but some stand up. All goalies play angles, and these goalies are no exception. They don't go down a lot. They stand, they usually are very good at playing angles, and the holes they give to shoot in are small. Grant Fuhr, who won four Stanley Cups with the Edmonton Oilers and is now with St. Louis, is a good example of a stand-up goalie.

A stand-up goalie concentrates on taking advantage of angles.

Dominik Hasek's Style: Anything Goes

Dominik Hasek, the goalie for the Buffalo Sabres and for the gold medal Czech Republic team in the 1998 Nagano Winter Olympics, doesn't have a definable style other than to call it his own. It is worth mentioning because he is so successful. Winning a gold medal for the Czech Republic is a phenomenal accomplishment. His style is that he just seems to go everyplace; he doesn't have a specific style but instead has a knack.

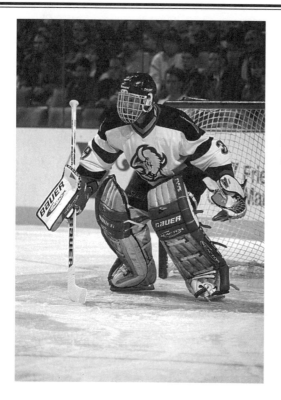

Dominik Hasek is a dominating goalie with a style all his own.

 ## CHEAP GOALS

Some shots are theoretically easy for an NHL goalie to stop. When a bad goal goes in, everybody knows it. Goalies don't like to let a soft shot float or slide in, and they certainly don't like to let something in from a corner when the goalie should rule the angle. Everybody recognizes a bad goal, especially the goalie who knows that everybody knows. For some goalies, that can be brutal. When a goalie lets in a "ten times out of ten I should stop this goal," it is a letdown for everyone.

For the Other Team

If you score a cheap goal off a goalie, it is like your birthday. Here is a present, and if it is a close game or a key goal, it is an especially nice present. And when it happens to the other team's goalie, well, it could not have happened to a nicer guy.

 ## HUGE SAVES

Some shots are automatic goals, until a goalie makes a superhuman effort. When a goalie does something sensational, so wildly improbable that it has everyone in the crowd either gasping, screaming, or clutching their hearts and blinking to check their eyesight, the change in flow is immense.

If you are a player and your goalie just made an unbelievable save, you are absolutely energized. And if you are at home, your body is in the business of manufacturing adrenaline because the crowd becomes absolutely insane, a rock concert frenzy without the guitars—plenty of drums, though. When a goalie makes a great save at home, the rhythm section goes wild. And players feed off it. A great save is essentially worth a goal. *They don't score!*

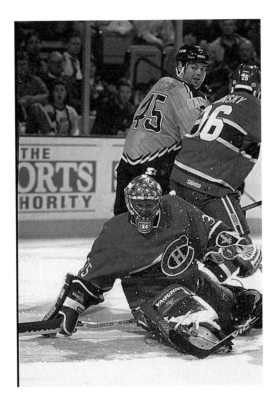

They don't score! A great save energizes the defense and deflates the offense.

For the Other Team

When some otherworldly talent saves your perfect shot, all you can think is: *Are you kidding me?*

You think you have a goal. You are already charging with the joy of accomplishment. Somehow the goalie in some kind of out-of-his-mind sprawl or dive or lunge manages to stop you and send your emotions crashing. Are you kidding me?

And the crowd reaction. If the goalie is at home, the crowd erupts with noise that reminds you overwhelmingly of what just happened. If the goalie is in your home rink, the crowd just collectively groans. Ouch.

WHEN A GOALIE IS HOT, SO IS THE TEAM

If a team doesn't have a good goalie, it isn't going anywhere in the NHL. A team has to have a good goalie to win and, in fact, a goalie can get hot at playoff time and win a series or two almost singlehandedly.

A team simply can't win the Stanley Cup without a great goalie who stays hot. If a great scorer gets cold, someone else on the team will pick up the scoring. But if the goalie gets cold, no one is there to pick up the slack. On the other hand, and I can't emphasize it enough, one great goalie can take a team a long way.

MY TOP 10 GOALIES

I began playing in the NHL in 1983 and have seen many great players. Here is a list, in no special order, of the 10 best goalies I have seen play since 1983.

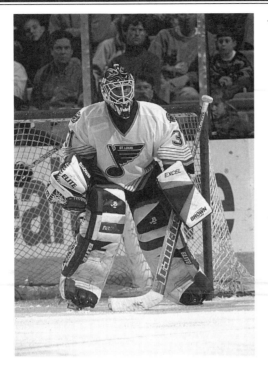

◀ ***Grant Fuhr*** Won five Stanley Cups with the Edmonton Oilers and is currently with the St. Louis Blues. He is a rare goalie because he catches with his right hand. Shooters have to shoot on the opposite side for the holes. He keeps playing solid year after year.

Andy Moog A teammate of mine in Boston, Moog won two Stanley Cups with Edmonton. He was a great goaltender who won a lot of big games and was very good at talking to his defense and helping them on the ice. He is also a great leader and encouraging in the locker room.

Patrick Roy Won two Stanley Cups with Montreal and one with Colorado. Roy is a legendary hero in Montreal who has carried some not-so-great teams extremely far in the playoffs.

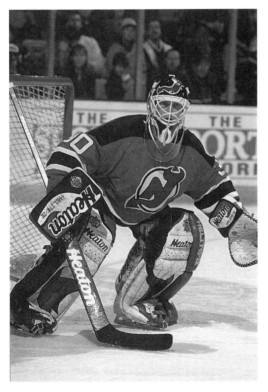

◀ ***Martin Brodeur*** Won the Stanley Cup with New Jersey. Brodeur is a big goaltender who covers a lot of the net. When a shooter looks at him and the goal, there doesn't seem to be anyplace to shoot. He is big in the net and he plays angles very well.

◀ ***Billy Smith*** Won four Stanley Cups with the New York Islanders, including his final one during my rookie year. Smith was one of the first goalies to become physically involved in front of the net. If you were in front of his net, you felt the lumber of his stick on the back of your legs. He protected his area.

John Vanbiesbrouck Played with the New York Rangers and is now with Florida. Vanbiesbrouck is the main reason why Florida went to the finals in 1996. He is a stand-up goalie who, although not tall, can cover the net.

◀ ***Mike Richter*** Plays with the New York Rangers, is very quick, plays the angles well, and is capable of going on a big run in the playoffs.

Sean Burke Played with New Jersey, Hartford (which moved to Carolina), Vancouver, and is currently with Philadelphia. Burke is a big goaltender who covers a lot of net. He has not always played with great teams so he doesn't get a lot of recognition, but he is a very solid goalie, especially in the late 80s and early 90s.

Mike Vernon Won two Stanley Cups, one each with Calgary and Detroit. A small man, he played as a big player and was known simply as a winner.

Dominik Hasek Playing with the Buffalo Sabres, is playing at an all-world level in 1998. If you get three goals on this guy, it's like getting six on someone else.

 ## FIVE GOALIES I CAN'T LEAVE OUT

Guy Hebert of Anaheim is a solid goaltender who, despite playing for an expansion team, plays better than the score sometimes indicates.

Nikolai Khabibulin of Phoenix is big goalie. It doesn't look as if there is much room to score on him.

Olaf Kolzig of Washington can win a game by himself. He has a great glove.

Felix Potvin of Toronto is a small goalie who is called "the cat" because he is extremely quick.

Curtis Joseph of Edmonton won a lot of games for Edmonton when the team was on the downside of its dynasty.

Strategies

In many ways, hockey strategy starts and ends with the ice surface of a player's youth. That's where hockey players learn their skills. Coaches are always trying to put those skills to the best use in their strategy. Thus, strategy grows from every local rink in the world.

In the NHL, all ice surfaces are the same. But all players are not the same. There is not a single Hockey Town where everyone first learns to play on the exact same rink. The great big hockey world out there has both big rinks and small rinks. In some parts of Canada and the United States, backyard rinks made by parents are common and there are always games on frozen ponds and lakes. Different rinks call for different strategies.

ONE OCEAN'S WORTH OF DIFFERENCE

The Atlantic Ocean is caught in the middle, a gulf between a continent of big rinks in Europe and the tradition of smaller rinks in North America. While there is no rule about styles of hockey, there are two clear and accepted generalizations:

1. North Americans play a rough, physical, dump-and-chase style of hockey because there isn't enough room to skate and control the puck.

2. Europeans play a more precise, puck-control style because they have more room to move and maintain control of the puck.

As in the case of most generalizations, there are exceptions—players who play with a style all their own. Yet these categories are a simple way to describe the two main strategies of NHL hockey, although a third, and arguably more popular strategy, is a mix of the two styles, a sort of hybrid strategy. After all, most teams have players from all over the world. Thus, hockey is a mixture of skills, strength, speed, savvy, and strategy. The reality is that players tend to develop differently on different ice surfaces and strategies develop to suit smaller or larger rinks.

In hockey's early days, the size of the ice surface was important in devising strategy. Now strategy revolves around the skills that players from different parts of the world have developed on different-sized ice surfaces and how to mix those skills together. Let's go for a quick world tour.

 ## NORTH AMERICAN STRATEGY

North American players tend to play physical. The style is a product of playing on smaller rinks where contact (between players and with the boards) is part of the game. As passing lanes are smaller, passing can sometimes be futile as a means of advancing the puck. Using this strategy, players will sometimes send the puck ahead and then go bang around and try to reach it before the other team gets control.

Dump the Puck

When there is an even strength 5-on-5 situation, it can be difficult to carry the puck into the offensive zone. There are too many bodies around. A player

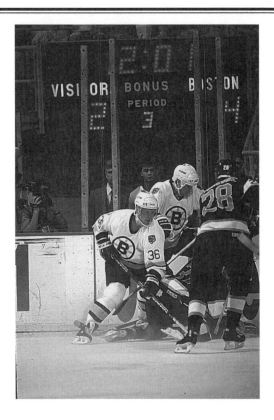

When the puck is dumped, the standard attack rule is that the first offensive player in will check the body of the opponent and the second offensive player will go after the puck.

may be able to pass it ahead but, more often than not, a team playing the North American style will dump the puck into the zone and then send three players charging at it.

There is a saying in hockey: Dump it hard or dump it smart. Dumping the puck into the other end is not a pass but rather a dump, a flick of the puck forward to no one. If you dump it hard, you dump it hard. If you dump it smart, you are careful. You dump it where your opponents probably can't get to it first. You put it in a place that makes it hard for the other team to have a lot of options for starting a play. Send it where one of your teammates is going and make the opposing defensemen turn around to chase it. Dump it to an area that keeps the puck away from the goalie. That is dumping it smart. If the opposing goalie gets to the puck, his team will almost certainly control it.

If You Don't Shoot, You Can't Score

Shots create opportunities, as long as the goalie doesn't catch or cover the puck. The typical North American strategy is to shoot early and often. The rule is—If you don't shoot, you can't score. Never on, never in.

As a shooter who played the North American style to its fullest extent, I knew that a puck bouncing around the crease could only be a good thing for the offense. As a guy who hung near the crease, I knew a shot on goal offered me a chance that the bounce might come my way. I had to be ready. When I had the puck, I shot. In the North American strategy, a shooter will usually shoot rather than pass in order to look for a better shot. The philosophy is that a better shot may never materialize, so shoot now and see what happens. But that's my feeling—passing was never my forte.

Playing Physical and Letting the Other Team Know It

In North America where the rinks are smaller, players simply run out of open room to skate. So they run into each other. It can be like bumper cars or a demolition derby depending on a million circumstances, but especially depending on the situation of the game—score and time.

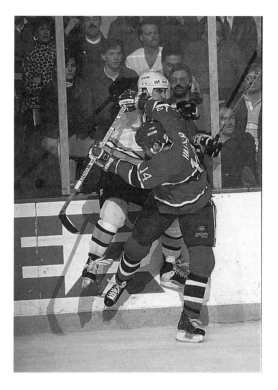

The North American strategy depends on teams playing physical and overpowering the other team.

The hits are not by accident. All NHL hockey players understand this. The idea is to establish territory and give the other player a message that there is a price to pay for any attempt to do things that don't meet your approval. *You want to go there? You want the puck? No, Don't go there. Get away from the puck! Cause I said so ...bam!* No need for words. Physical play is better than a speech and it is an essential part of North American strategy, a tough-minded, territorial, aggressive, burst-of-energy approach. Every hockey team, no matter the style of play, must use some degree of physical play.

 ## EUROPEAN STRATEGY

A bigger rink makes a big difference. Typically, the Europeans don't like to give the puck up and then chase it again. The strategy is different, not better or worse, just different. And when it works, it works quite well. Once a team gets control of the puck, the idea is to maintain control of the puck until a player can work out a way to get off a "perfect shot." The aim is to have a player open with a good angle on the goalie. Of course, the truth is that the only perfect shot is the one that goes in.

The European strategy calls for patience and precision. Work the puck, work the puck; take your time, move it, make slick passes, and then when someone breaks open—bang! A shot on goal. The aim is to work for a good, open shot.

The problem with this strategy in the NHL is that it calls for many "good" opportunities to be passed up in favor of the search for the "great" opportunity. If the great opportunity comes, then the strategy works. But often the great opportunity won't occur because the ice is smaller and there isn't enough time for multiple passing plays to develop. And, just as often, a great opportunity may develop off a good opportunity that was attempted. Hockey is not one play at a time. Hockey moves and flows; it is impossible to tell what could have happened if a player had shot instead of completing yet another European-style pass to try for the perfect shot. But, on the other hand, it often works.

Back in the 1960s and 1970s, the Soviet Red Army (the national team) epitomized the tic-tac-toe style of puck control. In international play, they overpowered other teams with their skilled passing.

Tic-Tac-Toe

Pass control can be amazing. Around and around to the point that the shooter literally has an empty net: Anybody could have made the shot. It is tic-tac-toe—quick, efficient passes that lead to one great scoring opportunity.

 ## HYBRID STYLE

Although teams tend to play one style more than the other, all teams in fact play a hybrid style of hockey that incorporates the skills and strategies of North America and Europe. The game of hockey is evolving.

Mixing the two strategies into a hybrid is somewhat essential in the NHL. Teams that try to play a European style almost always put a couple of physical players on the ice simply because hockey is a physical game. For a finesse line to work, someone has to be in the front playing physical. It will work better, of course, if the physical player is a good skater as well. But it is essential that at least one player on the line be a physical player.

On the other hand, teams using the North American strategy sometimes put a line of all physical players on the ice. Nevertheless, those teams will have some playmakers and skaters on their team to balance their attack. But at any given moment, a team using a North American strategy is not afraid to play with a power lineup.

Roles in Hybrid Hockey

As the hybrid style has developed, some hockey players have taken on various roles. Those players fine-tune their skills and make sure they carry out their roles. Strengths help the team.

Sure, hockey players work on their weaknesses, but they must remember that they are in the NHL because of their strengths.

A physical player who plays on a finesse team needs to continue to concentrate on his physical play. If the puck is dumped, the physical forward is the one to chase after it. He would take the hit. On the other hand, if it was dumped into the corner of the finesse forward, the finesse forward may not be as willing to mix it up. He may not go in there with the full intent of trying to knock the opponent off the puck. Instead, the finesse forward chasing a dump may only be trying to take the other player out of a play. The difference is a matter of intent and interpretation.

The physical player chasing the dumped puck goes in, gets a hit in, and tries to get the puck as well. He opens lanes for his finesse teammates. In theory, the combination of a physical player with two finesse players is powerful for this reason. Mixing skills is a path to success in the NHL. Of course, the key is the level of the players' skills. If you mix great players, there is a good chance that you'll get great results.

Traps

A new rage in the NHL is the trap defense, which tries to force the puck carrier to move the puck toward the boards as soon as he crosses his own Blue Line. As soon as he crosses, two players converge on him and he often cannot skate or pass through the assault. Sometimes the only option is to dump the puck down the ice. Some claim this strategy limits the offense and, in fact, since 1992 when the trap first came into vogue, scoring in the League has gone down by about one-third. The trap is very effective.

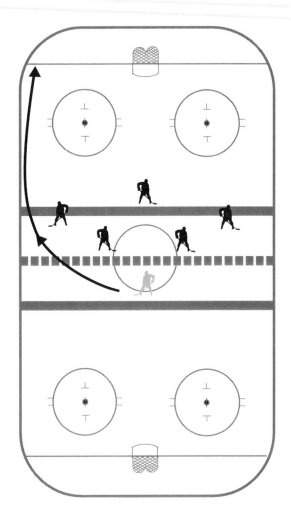

The trap defense cuts the puck handler off at his own Blue Line, forcing him toward the boards where two opposing players confront him.

Lock-Ups and Tracking

This hybrid mania has developed into a defensive strategy of keeping one wing so high that he is almost playing back. He acts as a lock, immediately ready to take any opposing player coming out of the other team's zone. Although this wing is involved in the offense when he gets a chance, his focus is altered a bit. He is a defensive lock on his side; he locks up the other player.

Another style used nowadays is called tracking. This means that the first man back in a transition from offense to defense plays a different role than normal. Instead of picking up the first forward without the puck, he will actually track down the puck carrier and try to force him to make a bad pass or a turnover. He doesn't give the puck carrier time to set up a play. He rushes at the puck carrier trying to force a quick decision that he hopes will not be a smart decision. I like this strategy.

The National Hockey League (NHL)

The pinnacle of the hockey world is the National Hockey League. Every player dreams of greatness, and those dreams always consist of playing in the NHL. It is the top. And at the very top of the top is the Stanley Cup championship.

This part of the book is about the NHL—the history, the playoff format, the business of the game, and the joy of just plain cheering for your favorite team. Here you will learn about some of the greatest players ever to play the game. The NHL has a rich lore, some intriguing and significant business rules, and a great playoff format that leads to the greatest of all championships: the Stanley Cup.

9

The Lore of the League

he history of NHL hockey is rich; the ice has layers of lore. Started as a league to compete with other leagues for the best hockey players in Canada, the National Hockey League has grown through a drumroll of great players into a financial and entertainment powerhouse. From the great ice barns of early-century Canada to the multimillion-dollar arenas of America's Sunbelt, the National Hockey League has matured along with modern society. And still, the game is hockey.

It has been and always will be the sport that is played brilliantly, roughly, toughly, with precision and aggression. Hockey flows, and hits, and flows. Sometimes it is swift and sometimes it is brutal. Hockey is many things to many people and there are so many details worth remembering that it is impossible to name them all. Here is a quick history lesson of some of the essentials.

ONCE UPON A TIME THERE WAS HOQUET

The French word for a shepherd's crook is *hoquet*. This may be the origin of the word hockey and the game that is played with a modified version of a shepherd's crook. It began as a version of field hockey and moved onto the ice in colder climates. By the 1840s, artificial ice was invented and, by the 1890s, the Canadian version of hockey had spread to the northern cities of the U.S.

Lord Stanley Buys a Trophy

In 1893 Lord Stanley of Preston, the sixth governor general of Canada and a devoted hockey fan, retired. That year, Lord Stanley bought a silver cup lined with gold as a challenge trophy for the hockey championship in Canada. It was named the Stanley Cup and quickly became the Holy Grail of hockey. Lord Stanley purchased the Cup for a little less than $50.

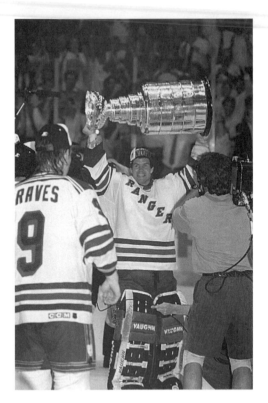

The Stanley Cup is awarded every year to the champions of the NHL.

Teams from all across Canada challenged each other for the Stanley Cup. Originally, the Cup was open to all challengers—there was no one league. There were leagues: rogue teams, challenging from all over; gypsy players or

In 1905, the Dawson City Klondikers overcame the most obstacles in Stanley Cup history in their challenge for the championship. The team from the Yukon had to take sleds pulled by dogs across miles of wilderness to reach the train that brought them east to challenge for the Cup. In between, they needed bicycles, stagecoaches, and a boat. Unfortunately for the Klondikers, after their 23-day journey they played against the legendary Ottawa Silver Seven led by Frank McGee. In the second game of the series, which Ottawa won, McGee scored 14 goals, a record that still stands.

mercenaries who sold themselves to the highest bidder, sometimes for as little as one game at a time. In its infancy, the challenge for the Stanley Cup had a bit of the Wild West feel to it. In fact, teams from 17 different leagues challenged for the Cup before it became the sole property of the National Hockey League in 1926.

Some of the First Heroes

Hockey had a number of stars in the years prior to the NHL, and here are a few of the most famous:

Fred "Cyclone" Taylor One of the first hockey players to realize the power of free agency, he barnstormed the United States in exhibitions that were packed due to his reputation. Taylor was a member of the famous Renfrew Millionaires, which was the best team money could buy in 1910. The Millionaires never won the Cup, but Taylor went on to win it playing for Vancouver in the Pacific Coast League.

◀ ***Edouard "Newsy" Lalonde*** A temperamental former lacrosse star who won scoring titles and played alongside Cyclone Taylor on the Renfrew Millionaires. Lalonde was picked up late in the 1910 season by the Millionaires but still scored 38 goals in 11 games.

◀ ***Georges Vezina*** A goaltender who played with the Montreal Canadiens from 1910 to 1925. Vezina came from the small lumber town of Chicoutimi, Quebec, and was so cool on the ice he was known as the Chicoutimi Cucumber. The Vezina Trophy is given to the goalie deemed best by a vote of NHL general managers.

Frank and Lester Patrick Founders of the Pacific Coast Hockey League, they added a number of innovations to the game including the Blue Lines, the crease, numbers on the jerseys, and the penalty shot. They also built the first artificial ice rinks in Canada. The Lester Patrick Trophy is given for outstanding service to hockey in the United States.

◀ ***Joe Malone*** A star scorer with the Quebec Bulldogs early in the century. He once scored nine goals in one game of a two-game Cup series (not all series were seven games back then).

Art Ross Won a Stanley Cup with the Kenora Thistles against the Montreal Wanderers, and the next year won a Cup with the Wanderers against the Thistles. Malone later won three Stanley Cups as coach and general manager of the Boston Bruins. The Art Ross Trophy is given to the player who leads the NHL in scoring during the regular season.

THE NHL IS BORN

On November 22, 1917, the National Hockey League was born as an alternative to other hockey leagues in Canada and as a way for a bunch of hockey men to start a league and hold a grudge. One owner in the new league described it to a reporter as "just like the National Hockey Association (an existing league) with one exception. We haven't invited Eddie Livingstone (owner of the NHA Toronto franchise) to be part of the setup." Another owner explained, "Livingstone was always arguing. Without him, we can get down to the business of making money."

And so this powerful grudge turned into a powerful enterprise—the NHL. Coincidentally, earlier that same year, the Seattle Metropolitans of the Pacific Coast Hockey League became the first American team to win the Stanley Cup, beating the Montreal Canadiens of the NHA.

The growth of the new league took a while. At first, the NHL was just another league trying to attract players and fans and make money on the growing popularity of this fast and brutal game. By 1926, the NHL took full control of the Cup and expanded the league to include the New York Rangers, Chicago Black Hawks, and Detroit Cougars. There were 10 teams that year.

Slowly, through the years, teams dropped out of the league until, by 1938, there were six teams left. The NHL stayed that way until 1967, when it expanded to 12. The six teams in the league from 1938-1967 are called The Original Six:

Boston Bruins   **New York Rangers**

Chicago Black Hawks   **Montreal Canadiens**

Detroit Red Wings   **Toronto Maple Leafs**

The original six are different from any collection of sports franchises as there are so few of them and they have stayed together for so long: six teams for all the hockey players in North America.

The Early Years

Getting a foothold in the United States was an important move for the NHL. The game of hockey was already a national passion in Canada when it began to make its way south. The timing was opportune as hockey entered the U.S. at the beginning of the golden age of sport, the 1920s. And hockey had its own set of heroes to compete with Babe Ruth and Jack Dempsey. In the northern cities of the United States, fans quickly caught the excitement.

Here are some of hockey's earliest heroes:

▶ **Howie Morenz** A quick charismatic scorer for the Montreal Canadiens. Morenz was able to bring fans to their feet with his adrenaline-pumping rushes up the ice. When he died shortly after a hockey accident, 250,000 in Montreal lined the funeral route to the cemetery.

Eddie Shore A tough energetic defenseman for the Boston Bruins who won the league MVP (most valuable player) four times. Shore once hit Irvin "Ace" Bailey of the Toronto Maple Leafs so hard that Bailey never played again.

Frank "King" Clancy This 150-pound defense-man built a lifetime career with the Toronto Maple Leafs. Clancy was known for having as much fun as anyone who ever played the game and often used conversation to get to his opponents.

Foster Hewitt The legendary Toronto Maple Leafs broadcaster who began calling games in 1926 was known for his *Hockey Night In Canada* broadcasts on Saturday nights as well as his signature call, "He shoots! He scores!"

Charlie Conacher A right wing of the Toronto Maple Leafs who was a scoring machine and part of the famous "Kid Line" featuring Joe Primeau at center and Harvey "Busher" Jackson at left wing.

Conn Smythe The first general manager of the New York Rangers who later bought the Toronto St. Pats and renamed them the Maple Leafs. Smythe was instrumental in the construction of Maple Leaf Gardens. When Smythe arrived in Toronto, he promised he would deliver a Stanley Cup within five years, and he delivered. The Conn Smythe Trophy is given to the most valuable player in the Stanley Cup playoffs.

The Original Six: Part One

The NHL plays a fast and brutal brand of sport that is not played anywhere else, and that was especially true in the three decades that preceded the great expansion of 1967. There were only six teams. This is phenomenal to think about; there are 26 teams today. The best players on some teams today could have trouble making one of only six teams. Back then, the players played without masks (even goalies for quite a while) and the battles were hard and furious. In the 1930s and 1940s, there were plenty of heroes in the NHL:

◀ *Milt Schmidt* A big strong playmaker who was the leader of Boston's famous "Kraut Line" along with Bobby Bauer and Woody Dumart. They were called the Kraut Line because they came from the German town of Kitchener, Ontario.

▶ *Maurice Richard* Right wing with the Montreal Canadiens, he was called "Rocket Richard." He is known as one of the best players ever from the Blue Line in, and he won eight Stanley Cups. Richard was almost possessed as he attacked the goal, and he scored 50 goals in a season for the first time.

Ted "Teeder" Kennedy Captain of the Toronto Maple Leafs, he led his team to five Stanley Cups. Ted was a great leader, strong on the face-off and a persistent battler.

Charlie Rayner Played with the New York Americans and then the New York Rangers. Rayner is the only goalie who ever scored a goal on an end-to-end rush. He was a big Hall of Fame goalie who got in the way of many shots.

The Original Six: Part Two

As hockey matured into the middle of the century, the NHL became a glamour sport in certain cities. The players were heroes on ice, and in their cities they were larger than life. World War II was over, there was peace and prosperity in most of the world, and the NHL was entering another golden era filled with wonderful stars.

◄ **Gordie Howe** Played with the Detroit Red Wings and was a hero of Detroit's Production Line that included Ted Lindsey and Sid Abel. Howe was a tough, mean hockey player and he played in the NHL until he was 52 years old. He was able to do things on the ice in an easy way that most players find hard. Howe dominated with power.

► **Ted Lindsay** Part of the Detroit Red Wing's "Production Line" and a great rival of Maurice "Rocket" Richard of the Montreal Canadiens. Lindsay was a great shooter and skater— a feisty hockey player.

Bernie "Boom Boom" Geoffrion Boom Boom was part of the five-in-a-row Montreal Canadiens dynasty in the 1950s, when the team won the Stanley Cup five consecutive years. He is best known for inventing the slap shot.

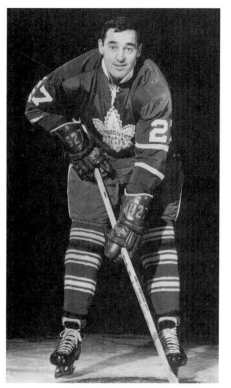

Frank Mahovlich A left wing with the Toronto Maple Leafs, Detroit Red Wings, and Montreal Canadiens, Mahovlich was known as "The Big M" because of his size and exciting abilities. He had a big slap shot and superb skating skills.

John Bucyk Known as "The Chief," Bucyk was a huge left wing for the Boston Bruins. He played hard and was known for his hip checks and his ability to play with power.

Jacques Plante Goalie of the Montreal Canadiens dynasty, Plante was the first modern goaltender to wear a mask.

Jean Beliveau Center of the Montreal Canadiens team that won five Stanley Cups in a row, Beliveau was a classy player as well as a great scorer and leader.

Stan Mikita Center with the Chicago Black Hawks, Mikita was a smart, nasty player who was a prolific scorer. He invented the "hooked" stick.

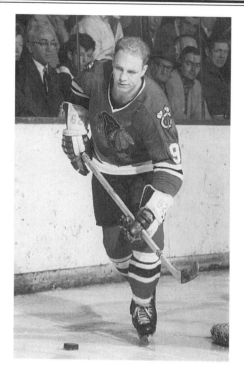

Bobby Hull Played with the Chicago Black Hawks and was known as the "Golden Jet" for his speed and his golden hair flying behind his head as he skated down the ice. Hull had a tremendous shot and great charisma. He was one of the renegade stars who joined the new World Hockey Association in 1972.

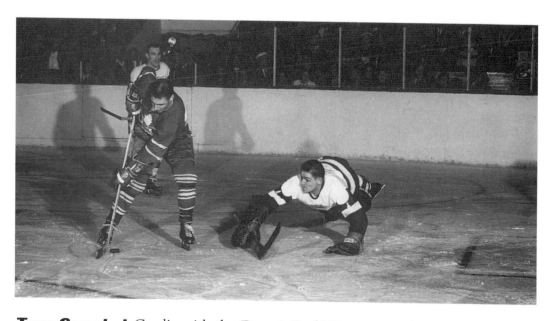

Terry Sawchuk Goalie with the Detroit Red Wings, Sawchuk was a standup goalie who was good with the glove and excellent at stopping rebounds.

Glenn Hall Goalie for the Chicago Black Hawks, Hall was the first to popularize the butterfly style. He was a reluctant goalie who once said of anyone who plays the position, "We're all a little bit sick."

▼ ***Henri Richard*** Number 16, known as the "Rocket's" brother or as "Pocket Rocket," in truth Henri won 11 Stanley Cups, five in a row. He was a star whose trophies said all that needed to be said.

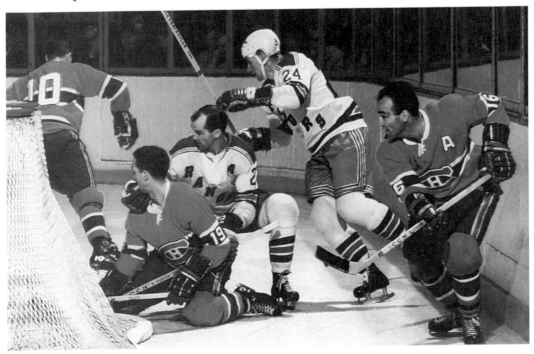

Expansion and Beyond: 1967 to 1983

There was money to be made in hockey and finally, in 1967, the NHL recognized the potential of its product and doubled in size, adding franchises in Los Angeles, Oakland, Minnesota, Philadelphia, Pittsburgh, and St. Louis. In 1970, the league again expanded, to Buffalo and Vancouver, and then in 1972, the league expanded again to Atlanta and Long Island (the New York Islanders).

In 1972, a new league sprung up to compete with the NHL—the World Hockey Association (WHA). By offering huge salaries to superstars such as Bobby Hull and Gerry Cheevers, the league gained instant credibility, although not on par with the NHL. The WHA lasted until 1980 when four teams—Edmonton, Hartford, Quebec, and Winnipeg—merged into the NHL. One of those teams, Edmonton, featured a young star named Wayne Gretzky. In 1981-82, Gretzky scored 92 goals in 80 games and had 120 assists for 212 total points. During this time, Gretzky was just beginning his career. Others players also stood out:

Bobby Orr The prototype rushing defenseman of the Boston Bruins who revolutionized the game with his multidimensional skills.

Phil Esposito A spectacular scoring center for the Boston Bruins, Esposito was a magician in front of the net—a specialist at getting tip-ins, deflections, and rebounds. He was a big player who couldn't be moved from the front of the net.

Guy Lafleur Right wing for the Montreal Canadiens, Lafleur played with spark and innovation. Using speed and a powerful shot, he had 50 goals a season for six consecutive seasons and won five Stanley Cups.

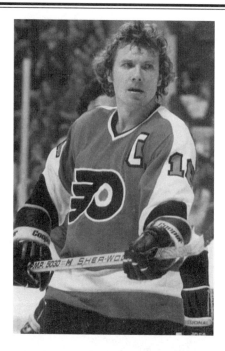

Bobby Clarke Center with the Philadelphia Flyers, Clarke was a tough, fiery leader famous for his photos showing two missing front teeth. Under his leadership, the Flyers were called "the Broad Street Bullies" and they won two Cups. They were the first expansion team to win a Cup.

Brad Park Defenseman for the New York Rangers and the Boston Bruins, Park was so intelligent and possessed such great puck control skills that he made an art of taking the puck backward, luring the forwards, and then making a perfect pass to start a break.

Lanny McDonald Right wing for Toronto, Colorado, and Calgary, McDonald was a fierce body checker and a prolific scorer. He was a big-game player.

Marcel Dionne Center with Detroit and Los Angeles, Dionne was a prolific scorer who had great speed and a very accurate shot.

Ken Dryden Goalie with the Montreal Canadiens, Dryden won six Stanley Cups and was a picture of calm under pressure.

Gerry Cheevers Goalie with the Boston Bruins, Cheevers was a fun-loving player capable of going on a great run, including an unbeaten string of 33 games in 1972. That year, he was one of the renegade stars who joined the new World Hockey Association.

MODERN TIMES: 1983 TO 1998

I began playing in 1983, so that is where I made the divide in this book. From 1983 on, hockey has grown tremendously. Salaries of superstars are now in nearly the same stratospheric air as those of other athletes. The NHL is a league of stars and action. Although some teams have been forced to move from Canada to bigger American cities, the game is stronger than ever. With an influx of many non-North American players, the game has grown and styles continue to mesh and evolve.

10

The Road to the Stanley Cup

Try imagining a place that is perfect. It is the pursuit of this place of momentary ecstasy that has brought all of us who have ever played professional hockey to respect the accomplishments of those who have won the Stanley Cup. It's why players do what they have to do in order to get a shot at it. Imagine being on that dogsled in 1905 (see Chapter 9) from Dawson City in the Yukon Territory, on the way to challenge for the Stanley Cup. Now, more than 90 years later, teams are thriving in the desert of Arizona as well as in the tropics of southern Florida—and still hoping for a shot at the Cup.

If you are a hockey player (or fan), your perfect hockey future involves one thing—the Stanley Cup in your city. Whether you are from Dawson City and send your team away on a dogsled or whether you are from the Sunbelt and send your team away on a chartered jet in 1998, you send them away for only one thing: to win the Cup.

THE BASIC SETUP

At the end of the 1997–98 season, there were 26 teams divided into two conferences: the Eastern and Western Conferences. Each conference was divided into two divisions.

In 1998, a new team, the Nashville Predators, joined the NHL and the league has now split each conference into three divisions:

Eastern Conference

Northeast Division	Atlantic Division	Southeast Division
Boston Bruins	New Jersey Devils	Carolina Hurricanes
Buffalo Sabres	New York Islanders	Florida Panthers
Montreal Canadiens	New York Rangers	Tampa Bay Lightning
Ottawa Senators	Philadelphia Flyers	Washington Capitals
Toronto Maple Leafs	Pittsburgh Penguins	

Western Conference

Central Division	Northwest Division	Pacific Division
Chicago Black Hawks	Calgary Flames	Anaheim Mighty Ducks
Detroit Red Wings	Colorado Avalanche	Dallas Stars
Nashville Predators*	Edmonton Oilers	Los Angeles Kings
St. Louis Blues	Vancouver Canucks	Phoenix Coyotes
		San Jose Sharks

*Expansion team in 1998–99

HOW THE PLAYOFFS WORK NOW

Eight teams in each conference make the playoffs. First, the winners of each of the three divisions in the conference get to go to the playoffs. After that, the five teams with the best regular season record also get to go.

Details, Details, Details!

Playoffs work this way:

The three division winners in each conference are seeded 1, 2, 3. The team with the most points is ranked 1. The remaining five playoff teams in each conference are seeded based upon regular season points.

Team record is based on points, a concept unique to hockey, and is not used in the three other major sports. The reason is that in the NHL regular season, there are ties.

A win is worth 2 points.
A tie is worth 1 point.
A loss is worth zero points.

At the end of the season, the team with the most points has the best record.

Matchups work this way (numbers refer to seeded teams):

8 plays 1
7 plays 2
6 plays 3
5 plays 4

The teams play a best-of-seven series—meaning whichever team wins four games advances. Once there are four winners, the highest remaining seed plays the lowest remaining seed. Then there are two teams left in the conference. They play each other for the right to play in the Stanley Cup finals. The opponent will be a team that went through the same process in the other conference.

Who Plays When and Where

All series are best of seven—with four games played in one city and three in the other. In almost all cases, the series is played on a 2-2-1-1-1 basis—meaning that the higher-seeded team gets the first two games at home and then the fifth and seventh game at home.

The only exception occurs when a Central Division club plays against a Pacific Division Club (because of time differences and jet lag). In such a series, the higher-ranked club can make a choice:

> **2-2-1-1-1**
>
> **or**
>
> **2-3-2**

If the 2-3-2 series is selected, the higher-ranked club will also have choice of playing games 1 and 2, and 6 and 7 at home or playing games 3, 4, and 5 at home. That option is in place in the first three rounds only, not in the finals.

It Is Good to Win Your Division

Division champions rank higher than non-division winners in all conference playoff games, even when non-division winners have more regular season points.

When Two Teams Are Tied

In the event of two or more clubs tied in points at the conclusion of the season (and one of them is not a division champion), the standing of the clubs in the conference ranking will be determined in the following order:

1. Most games won.

2. Higher number of points earned in games against each other. If two clubs are tied and have not played an equal number of home games against each other, points earned in the first game played in the city that had the extra game shall not be included. If two or more clubs are tied, the higher percentage of available points earned in games among those clubs shall be used to determine the standings.

3. The greater differential between goals scored for and against during the entire regular season.

In the Finals

The home ice will be determined by the higher number of regular season points subject to the tiebreaker procedure above. Division winners do not get precedence over regular season points in the finals. Games will be played on a 2-2-1-1-1 basis.

Expansion Is Coming

The League is now up to 27 teams for the 1998 season. In 1999, there will be a new team in Atlanta that will join the Southeast Division. In 2000, the Columbus Bluejackets will join the Central Division and the Minnesota Wild will join the Northeast Division—giving the league a total of 30 teams for the 2000–2001 season.

REGULAR SEASON HOCKEY IS DIFFERENT FROM PLAYOFF HOCKEY

The season can go on and on until sometimes one game blends into another. But as the season progresses and there is a clear end in sight, things begin to change. The last 10 or 15 games begin to feel different. All games count equally, of course, in the absolute logical sense. But at the end of the season, games seem to count more. When there are fewer games left and when the season has already put every team in some position or other in the standings, each game remaining is worth more than a game early in the season when teams have not yet established a course and direction.

The message is drilled into hockey players: The fifth game of the season is just as important as the 75th. That's the game that could make the difference in the season. Each game is important. Players know it and try their hardest at all times. All athletes should take pride in the job they do, pride in their performance, and pride in their team. If an athlete takes a game as just another game, it will show in his or her performance. Professional hockey players play professional hockey—at the highest levels humanly possible.

At the end of the season when the stakes are raised and opportunities are fewer, the intensity level is naturally higher. Players hit harder, skate cleaner, pass sharper, and focus better. The level is so high that it would be impossible for a player to maintain playoff intensity level throughout the season. No matter how intense a player is during the season, he picks it up a notch toward the end and then it goes up again in each level of the playoffs.

 ## LOSERS GO HOME AND THAT'S FINAL

When the season is over and you qualify for the playoffs, you could have anywhere between 4 and 28 games left. The road will end. The question is, will you make it all the way? Only one team will make it. If your team makes it, no other team does. How sweet is that? I wish I knew. We went two trips to the big dance (the finals), and lost both times to the Edmonton Oilers. So close has never felt so far away.

The potential disappointment grows with each success you have. If you don't make the playoffs, for instance, you're disappointed and maybe even angry but, in the end you know you have next season to move forward. If you are eliminated in the first round of the playoffs, it sure would have been nice to go further. The closer you get and don't win, the more you are reminded that

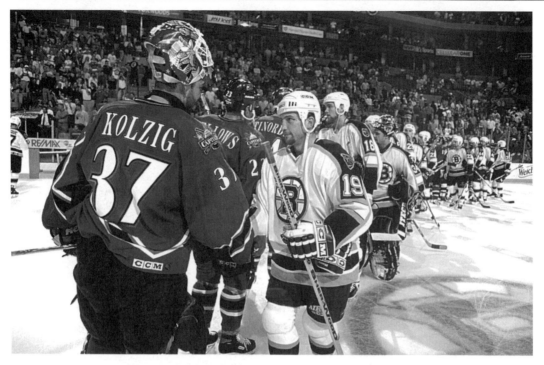

It is never easy for a season to end without a championship.

you are not going to win the Stanley Cup. The closer you get, the more you can taste it. So close and then nothing! Each and every year that realization hits for almost every hockey player. Wait till next year.

In the playoffs, the pressure is amazing. There's an exponential growth in intensity as teams advance from series to series until, finally, in the Stanley Cup finals, players are playing at historic levels.

The playoffs are so final. You may have not lost four games in a row all season. And now if you lose four of the next seven, you are gone. This happens in every round during the playoffs. Lose four out of seven in any round and it's over. And the farther you go, the harder it is to deal with ultimate failure. When almost really becomes almost, it stays with you for a long time.

PLAYOFF HOCKEY BY THE NUMBERS

It is important to win the first game of a playoff series, especially if you are the home team. The first two games are played at home; you have home ice advantage (meaning four games are at home and three are away). The emotional lift from the home crowd is important and teams are careful to take advantage of it. The first game sets a tone and gives all players and coaches something to build on and remember going into game two. The first game is huge and the outcome sets a number of things in motion. The winning team, obviously, knows they only need three more wins, while the losing team suddenly realizes its chances of winning the series just went down.

But some also say that winning game three is just as important because it's the first game in a new arena. It can change momentum in a series. This is a pivotal game due to changing venues as well as the stage of the playoff series (either one team is winning 2–0 or the series is tied 1–1.

Sometimes, series begin to shift one way or another. A team may take a 3–0 lead in games. Or a team may fall behind by that much. I have been in both situations. When you are up 3–0 and you lose, you may be on home ice and you have to go to the other team's rink. So, you are up 3–1 going to the other team's rink and you realize it is tougher to win there. You get a little nervous. If you lose you think, now it's 3–2 and if we lose the next one, we have to come back to their arena for a seventh game. The point I'm trying to make is that if you are up 3–0, you can't take it easy. You absolutely cannot give the other team any life. Zero. When they are down, you want to kick them—hard.

It works the same way from the downside of 3–0. The mountain seems huge. There has been no success so far. But players know, they just know, that if they can get one victory in, they can get something going. Change the momentum. Let the other team know they are in for a battle. Once the scare is in, weird things can happen.

The key, of course, is focus. Players must develop a sort of tunnel vision to the task at hand. If you have won 12 playoff games, don't think ahead to the 16 it takes to win the Cup. You must only think of wining game 13. The focus must be complete because the team that has that focus becomes the champion.

For some teams, especially teams that make the Stanley Cup finals for the first time, there can be a feeling of accomplishment of just playing in the finals. Wow, we're playing in the finals! That's how it was the first year my team, the Bruins, went to the finals in 1988. The majority of us had never been there before. The second time, in 1990, even though we lost again, was more of job for us. The dreamlike quality of playing in the Stanley Cup finals had worn off a bit. And even though we couldn't turn the corner, many teams have found that they need to fail on the last step before they come back the next year to ultimately win the Cup. After you've been to the finals and lost, you realize just making it to that series is not anywhere near satisfying enough. What you don't realize at the time of your first experience in the finals is the uncertainty of whether you will ever get back to the finals again. Players should understand this may be a once-in-a-lifetime experience and make the most of it.

 ## LET ME TAKE THE SHOT

Some people want to accomplish more than they can, but at least they keep trying. I admire them. Others could accomplish more than they do, but they don't try hard enough. It's just too much work when they can be satisfied and comfortable with mediocre accomplishments. That's how it is in life, and that's how it is in the NHL.

It is just your personality. It depends what you want to do. Greatness is accomplished on the outside but, in many ways, it comes from within. I know that when I played I liked to be the guy that got the big goal. I lived for that. I loved that. I knew I could fail, but I believed I would succeed. I wanted to take the chance.

When you can accomplish what people expect you to accomplish, you do it year after year. It makes your confidence grow. It is like watching Michael Jordan at the end of a game. Everyone on both teams, in the arena and in the television audience, knows he is going to take the shot. So he does and most of the time he makes it. Most people expect him to make it. He is the man, never afraid to take the chance. For me, when it came to crunch time and we needed a goal, my attitude was simply this: *I want to get that goal.*

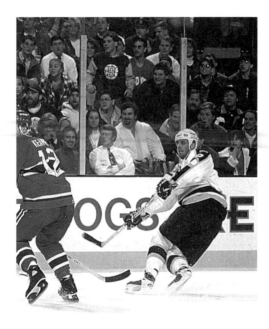

When it comes to a big shot, some players shy away while others think, I want to get that goal!

WINNING IT ALL

I never won a Stanley Cup, but I've seen it done on television. In fact, I've watched Cups won up close—twice. The grand display plays out the same year after year. Every player who doesn't win watches the events with a bit of envy. If only...

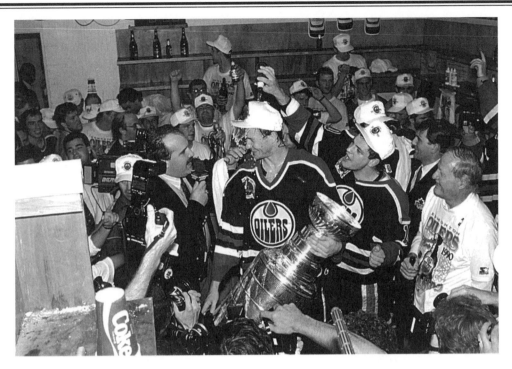

Winning is the greatest feeling!

The winning captain picks up the Cup and skates around the perimeter of the ice. And every player touches it, carries it. Around the rink, grand and glorious. All players who play in the NHL dream of this moment, carrying the Cup in the home rink and then drinking from the Cup in a great gesture of camaraderie and accomplishment. Victory!

I won a championship in junior hockey so I've seen the territory. It may not have been the gilded land of the Stanley Cup, but it was still sweet. There is just nothing like winning the last game of the year in a team sport. If you are a champion in an individual sport, people pat you on the back and say "Great job!" But it's not the same as in a team sport—it's not the same as in hockey.

Celebrating with teammates is an unbelievable feeling. You look across the rink and see a guy who has six stitches above his eye and a busted nose, another guy with teeth missing, and other players with bruises and hurts. But you made it! Together. You're feeling hurt, you're banged up with sweat pouring off you and you've been doing this for a whole season plus the playoffs. Finally you know that you are there. Was it worth it? You bet. No professional hockey player would pass up the chance to drink from the Cup. Victory. Ultimate victory belongs to champions. When you win, you finally understand.

The Business of Hockey

Professional hockey is a sport and, like all professional sports, it is part of the entertainment industry. In other words, there is a lot of money involved. These huge sums of money that seem to grow year by year have put the spotlight on hockey. Money has transformed the game of hockey into a level of entertainment approaching the three major sports—baseball, basketball, and football. As the game on the ice has evolved, so has the game off the ice. And off the ice, hockey is clearly a business—a big business.

The interesting part is that the action on the ice is starting to be affected by what happens off the ice. Money can try to buy wins, and it can try to buy championships. But the talent that money buys must still possess the heart and magic that make up a championship team. Other teams have talent too. The stuff of championships is not bottled. It is not sold. Hockey at its professional core is still hockey—a red-hot game on ice. In the middle of it all, no player should be thinking of money.

Money should not be a subject for players until their contract is up. Players, however, realize hockey is big business to the team owners. As players, we never dreamt of making this kind of money to play hockey. There is more focus on the business side of hockey nowadays because (1) the money involved is getting increasingly larger and (2) players understand that their bodies will only hold up for a limited time.

MONEY, MONEY EVERYWHERE

On the periphery of the game, everyone is thinking about money. Entertainment dollars across the land are astronomical! Hockey, left behind in the early days of the entertainment gold rush, is catching up quite nicely. There are a lot of people who play hockey (and who don't play hockey) who are getting rich off the NHL. Yet the NHL still lags behind Major League Baseball, the NBA, and the NFL (baseball, basketball, and football respectively) in terms of revenues and player salaries. Hockey is growing rapidly, yet there is still more room for growth.

As the sport of hockey journeys into the Sunbelt and as rollerblading exposes youngsters to the game in unprecedented numbers, there is more enthusiasm for the game and the audience grows. More people watching means more revenue for everybody.

Rollerblading (also called in-line skating) is gaining popularity across North America and is bringing the game of hockey to those who may not live near an ice rink. According to the National Sporting Goods Association, roller hockey participation is up 123 percent in the 7 to 11 age group and up 46 percent in the 12 to 17 age group.

Audience, of course, is the key to any entertainment business. Hockey is an interesting study because hockey fans are probably the most passionate of all sports fans. Yet hockey is in fourth place in terms of popularity in North America. The reason, at least to hockey fans, is clear.

The people who have really been exposed to hockey—those in Canada and the northern United States—love the game more than any other. Hockey's fourth-place ranking is only temporary while the NHL spreads the word to the rest of the sporting world. Once the folks who live in the heat catch on to the excitement, the red-hot game on ice cannot help but capture their attention. Go to a game. You'll see. It's the game of the next millennium.

Some numbers back this up. According to the NHL:

- More U.S. boys ages 7 to 14 living in NHL team markets named hockey as the sport they would most prefer to play, with 44 percent saying they prefer hockey over basketball, football, baseball, and soccer.

- There was an 87.5 percent increase in viewership of the NHL on ESPN among male teens 12 to 17 years old during the first quarter of the 1997–98 season.

- There was a 75 percent increase in viewership of the NHL on ESPN among female teens 12 to 17 years old during the first quarter of the 1997–98 season.

- Since USA Hockey began tracking female participation during the 1990–91 season, female membership has increased 308 percent and the number of girls' and women's teams registered has increased 511 percent.

- In Canada, the number of female hockey registrants has grown 288 percent over the past 10 years, which is understated since female players are not required to state gender on registration forms. These numbers do not reflect all female teams at various levels.

"Hockey generates an enthusiastic and relatively young audience," Peter McLoughlin, group director of corporate media for Anheuser-Busch, told *NHL FAN* magazine. It's true. Hockey is something anyone interested in making money will want to invest in. It's very hot. According to *NHL FAN:*

- Hockey is the favorite sport of households with annual incomes of more than $50,000.

- Hockey is the favorite sport of those with a college education.

- Hockey is the favorite sport of men 18 to 34.

- Hockey is the favorite sport of those who categorize themselves as Professional/Executive/Administrator/Manager.

 ## TELEVISION AND HOCKEY

The puck is small and on most television screens—very small. But from the stands, even from far away, the action somehow translates.

Television often uses the strategy of giving fans the up-high perspective. This view allows fans to observe a play develop, an educational process. Television coverage of the game has really evolved in recent years and the FOX channel has instituted blue streaks and red streaks to indicate when the puck is shot fast and really fast. Although some hardcore hockey fans don't like the streaks, they do add something to the broadcasts for casual fans. Almost everyone likes the miles-per-hour graphic on slap shots.

Hockey coverage is evolving and getting better. Not all experiments work, but people who are exposed to the game become fans. Fast, fun, furious. Hockey rules, but yet television rules. A major reason why hockey is behind the other three sports in terms of revenue is that hockey doesn't get as much national network and cable coverage. It's simple: Television equals revenue.

The popularity of hockey in general is increasing, due in large part to television exposure. The NHL is now broadcast on the CBC in Canada, and FOX,

ESPN, and ESPN2 in the U.S. In fact, the contract with FOX, signed September 20, 1993, was the first broadcast network contract for the NHL in almost 20 years. Remember, television equals revenue.

Hockey is growing not only in North America, its growth is a global phenomenon. Live or repeat broadcasts of NHL games are now seen twice a week in more than 160 countries, including China, England, Italy, Mexico, and Spain.

 ## PLAYERS AND TEAMS

Professional hockey is not like most jobs. Anyone who reads the sports pages understands that. Hockey is a short and risky career that generates a great deal of consumer interest and, therefore, revenue. High stakes are often gambled on the prospect of future results. Issues of money can become heated between players and teams. Some teams (and some players) handle it better than others. But all have to handle it; it is an integral part of the game.

One of the biggest issues for both sides is player movement from team to team—free agency. Free agency means players and teams get together and choose each other. Even trades are sometimes made because players are about to become free agents at the end of a particular season. But free agency in hockey is quite restricted compared to other sports. So, what is free agency?

First-time employees in professional hockey, for the most part, get drafted. Players are picked each year (the worst team picks first) and are given no choice as to where they play. This is the same as in most professional sports leagues. The NHL draft consists of nine rounds, which means that each team is given nine picks, one in each round. Those picks, as you will learn later, are often given to other teams before the draft occurs. In each draft, some teams choose more players and some choose less. But there are still nine rounds, with one pick originally allocated to each team in each round.

Think of it this way: In your job, if someone offers you more money to do the same job at another company, you would most likely leave your current employer and go to the higher bidder. If you did this, you would be taking advantage of free agency in your profession.

It's a little more complicated in hockey. In the NHL, you have to earn the right to be a free agent. You earn it by paying with time. Players, in many respects, are property. Teams own them. And, like all smart businesses, teams don't like to let their property go to another owner without some compensation. Thus, the NHL and the National Hockey League Player's Association (NHLPA) have negotiated a Collective Bargaining Agreement (CBA), which sets the rules about when players are allowed to leave their teams. Not all players are allowed to become free agents. The CBA rules set a number of categories:

Group I—First Player Contract

This category includes all players under the age of 25 who are playing for their first professional contract. Not all of these contracts are of the same length—the length of the contract actually depends upon the age of the player when he signed it.

Standard First Contract

Age Signed	Length of Contract
18 to 21	3 years
22 to 23	2 years
24	1 year

All players in these age groups in their first contract are Group I players. Pay limits for Group I players are set to keep salaries down to an even scale for new players. The big money (for the good players) comes after the first contract is finished. The longer a player has been in the league, the more freedom he has to put himself on the open market.

Group II—Restricted Free Agents

The first step towards free agency is not exactly complete freedom. In the NHL, players must meet certain qualifications to become restricted free agents. First, they cannot be a Group I or Group IV player (playing in a non-NHL-affiliated league).

If they are not an unrestricted free agent, they must meet the following qualifications to be a restricted free agent.

Restricted Free Agent Contract

First Contract Signing Age	Eligible For Group II
18 to 21	3 years professional
22 to 23	2 years professional
24 or older	1 year professional

Players younger than 20 do not earn a year of professional service unless they have played 10 or more games in the NHL during a given season. All players older than 20 earn a year of professional service for playing NHL or minor league professional hockey.

But what is a restricted free agent? A restricted free agent is a player who can sign with another team, but his original team has the right to match the offer. Additionally, if the original team does not match the offer, the team that signed the player must compensate the original team with draft picks. In other words, if you sign a restricted free agent and his team doesn't match, it will cost you future draft picks. How many picks? Well, that depends on how much you pay your new player.

Draft Pick Compensation for Restricted Free Agents

Offer	Draft Picks
$400,000 or below	None
Over $400,000 to and including $550,000	Third Round
Over $550,00 to and including $650,000	Second Round
Over $650,000 to and including $800,000	First Round
Over $800,000 to and including $1 million	First and Third Round
Over $1 million to and including $1.2 million	First and Second Round
Over $1.2 million to and including $1.4 million	Two First Rounds
Over $1.4 million to and including $1.7 million	Two First Rounds and One Second Round
Over $1.7 million	Three First Rounds
Each additional million	Additional First Round Pick up to a maximum Five First Round Picks

What about unrestricted free agents? Unrestricted free agents can sign with any team upon completion of their existing player contract. It's just like most jobs.

Group III

This category includes any player at the conclusion of his player contract who fulfills the following:

1. Has played at least four NHL Seasons
2. Is 31 years of age or older as of June 30, for League Years 1997–98 through 1999–2000

These players are completely free to negotiate a player contract with any team.

Group IV

This category includes any player in a non-NHL-affiliated league.

Group V

This category includes any player at the conclusion of his player contract who fulfills the following:

1. Has played 10 professional seasons
2. Earned less than the league average salary in the last year of his expired contract
3. Has not previously made a Group V selection.

These players may elect to become an unrestricted free agent and are free to sign with any other team.

Group VI

This category includes any player at the conclusion of his contract who fulfills the following:

1. Is 25 years of age or older
2. Has not played in 80 NHL games (for goaltenders, 28 games)

These players may elect to become an unrestricted free agent and are free to sign with any other team.

 ## LOYALTY

It happens—I've seen it happen. Players start in a city or come to a city to play hockey. Then the fans and, in some ways, the city begin to support that individual. It's an unbelievable feeling that works both ways. Fans love it, obviously. Players love it more.

I have seen players come to a city and then start a family. Sometimes it means more to the player to raise their youngsters in a city their kids are comfortable in rather than chase every last dollar. This is especially true for players who are nearing the end of their career. It is worth staying for a player to keep his family in comfortable surroundings.

The connection of a player and a city when things are on a roll is great. I was lucky enough as a player to go on a few of those rolls. It was special, indescribable. And, just by watching, I've seen it from the other side as a fan. It's fantastic. We're all cheering. Being on a roll is great.

 ## PAYING THE BILLS

Players understand that although fans pay the bills, fans don't make the decisions. The 20,000 people in the arena do not make the business decisions for the team. They only approve them.

What Really Happens

I think that, after a certain period, a player begins to like where he has landed. In fact, that is what has happened—through the draft or through a trade. You land. And, if you are lucky (as I was) you land in a great city.

If you are not traded and your contract is up, and if you have been with a team for a while and have put down roots, you begin to think that maybe this is a good place. And then somehow money doesn't matter as much. Of course, it always helps when there are at least two big numbers to choose from. Then, it is sometimes okay to choose the smaller of the big numbers. The truth is that no team can guarantee anything but money. Winning can never be bought. Talent, however, is for sale. But the highest bidder doesn't always win.

 ## FRANCHISE FREE AGENCY

Teams move. Teams are born and then exist and then move. Usually the move is about money. Some cities simply cannot support an NHL franchise. Yet others may not be able to keep one because they are in the far northern reaches of Canada. It's unfortunate because hockey is the sport in Canada. It is sad, yet the owners are looking at a business decision—where is the best place to make money?

While the team owners are fans, they also have millions and millions of dollars invested. Sometimes, they see the pot of gold at the end of the rainbow. Most recently, it's been in the south.

Here is a recent sampling of NHL moves:

- Minnesota North Stars became Dallas North Stars—1993

- Quebec Nordiques became Colorado Avalanche—1995

- Winnipeg Jets became Phoenix Coyotes—1996

- Hartford Whalers became Carolina Hurricanes—1997

 ## THE COMPETITIVE NATURE OF MONEY

Teams have to be careful who gets their money. Not every player plays night in and night out like clockwork. Teams are very careful about who gets the big money. Teams understand. They ask questions, they ask people around the player. They don't just look at statistics.

I would rather have a guy on my team who is always playing hard, even if he doesn't produce the greatest numbers. A flashy guy who might not show up and play hard on any given night is a very difficult player to have on a team. You never know what you are going to get. Some players play hard all the time. Some don't. Some are not willing to always go the extra step, take the extra hit. It is a passion for most of us. But some have demonstrated that to them, it's just a job.

It all comes out in the playoffs. That's when a year's worth of habits show up, when people show their true colors. Everything is intensified and, despite all the money in the world, hockey is still just a red-hot game on ice. We all play to win the championship of the ultimate team sport. We all play for the Stanley Cup.

12

Cheering with Friendly Abandon

Some things in life are simple and the simple fact is that hockey is the greatest game in the world, which every player understands. But a passion for hockey is not just for the players. Hockey is for the fans too. As the fans react to our game, we react to your reaction. And if we're on my home rink, well, thanks for the energy.

When the game is on the ice, there is a connection between players and fans. Players feel the responsibility of fan loyalty and give it back—loyalty is a two-way street in the world of hockey. Players and fans are on the same page; that's one of a million things that makes hockey great.

Fans have enjoyed hockey for years in arenas across North America (and around the world) and on television. Maybe it depends on the team you root for, but I know many hockey fans who are fanatical about their team. These are great people. They understand the game and have a lot of fun being fans. And it's just like hockey—they get better with practice.

COME ALONG FOR THE RIDE

It is a vicarious vocation—hockey fan. To cheer or not to cheer is not the question. The question is more like: Do you like what just happened on the ice? Do you think you, or any of your friends or neighbors or even the guy that was on the team last year—do you think anybody could do better? Although there is no legal commitment by the fan when the ticket is purchased, there is a hockey-fan commitment. Watch the action. Absorb the energy and help it grow. Voice your approval, or disapproval, as the situation on the ice may warrant.

The players know about you. Out on the ice where they are working hard, sweating, and maybe hurting, they know that you paid good money to see them play and they will play with full intensity. They see you up there in the stands, some of you wearing the same hockey sweater. Players understand what it is to be a fan because almost all started out as a fan of some team themselves.

So join! The season is long, the playoffs are intense, and the whole experience of NHL hockey is something to be cherished and shared by fans and players. Years from now, we can all say to each other, Do you remember when...?

It Starts with Attitude

Although many hockey fans enjoy attending games and sitting quietly in the stands, hockey is not typically a game for the shy. Hockey fans have, in fact, been known to be a bit boisterous from time to time. Hockey fans scream.

This is especially true in Boston, where I played. Boston is a passionate sports town with a passionate group of fans, similar to a lot of cities. Fans have their own routines and superstitions, just like the players. As fans live vicarious sports lives through the players, they often develop game-day routines that hold great powers. Every fan knows it. Superstition lives. The way you put your socks on at home on game day could affect how your goalie will play that night.

Fans yell and roar and shout and clap and pound. They scream and cheer in the same way the game is played—all out. Players were once fans and know that fans understand the fire inside that is needed to play in the NHL. Players know that fans understand the fire because fans throw it at the players in every NHL rink. The sound of a hockey game is a roar.

It starts with attitude. It is wonderful to see fans come into the arenas with a knowledge of the game and a passion for the events on the ice. Fans who come into an arena with confidence about their team are able to transfer their confidence to others and then, during the game, onto the home team. They are even able to transfer the energy to the visiting team too. That's when things get interesting.

Into the Lion's Den

There are a lot of opportunities for players and fans to interact over the course of a season and then during the playoffs. It is always interesting to go to another city to play a game. I could tell the difference between the screamers and the loudmouths and the wild-eyed true believers and yet it didn't matter, they all yelled against us. *Hey Neely, you suck!*

It was common and it was all right because they mostly yelled at the best players. It gave me energy. If the opposing fans had realized that, they may have stopped—but probably not. It is their only way to compete in an NHL game and they give it their all. The best part is that—negative or positive—the fans do have an effect.

What Happened to That Guy in the Stands?

Sometimes, the situation can be funny. I remember one game in New York against the Rangers when a loudmouth yapped at me all game. It was great. On and on he went, informing the world that his opinion of my hockey skills did not meet his high standards, although he didn't exactly say it that way. He got on me quite a bit as the game wore on and I hadn't scored. We were losing the game 2 to 1 and he was really riding me. Well, I scored the tying goal and in overtime helped set up the winning goal. I don't think I'll ever forget that particular fan in New York. Sometimes, it's hard not to hear the fans and I certainly heard him.

The Lion's Den at Home

There are no fans like hometown fans. When a team is at home, fans are rabid and let the team know that they have much more than mere hope for victory. They expect it. It is wonderful to play in front of hometown fans who cheer every move as if it were part of some revolution or a grand civic drama. But if things go wrong…

Hockey fans are emotional. They take the game seriously and certainly have the right to expect players to play their hardest. But sometimes, hockey fans can be downright harsh. And even then, it's okay. Those seats cost a lot of money and the players make a lot of money. Fans have the right to expect a lot. They can make the home arena the most uncomfortable place in the world for a team that is struggling. Most hockey fans are fair but tough.

Although some fans may have a lot of knowledge, the ticket doesn't make anyone an expert. Yet some fans act as if it does, and that's fine. Come and cheer and boo and do your part to make NHL hockey exciting. Hockey is about competition and the atmosphere of competition. You are part of the atmosphere. Players love it and other fans love it. Energy feeds on itself. Go to a hockey game. You'll see.

So That's What 50 Goals Means Now!

One year after one of my 50-goal seasons, we played Hartford in the first round of the playoffs. We lost the first game something like 5 to 2 and as we went off the ice, one of our fans yelled, *Hey Neely, 50 goals means nothing now, does it?*

It's fine for fans to get involved, but that particular incident was a little disheartening. We were at home and I knew I hadn't helped my team as I could have that game. But I knew that six games remained in the series. In fact, in the second game I scored a hat trick and we went on to win the series!

ROOTING FOR THE HOME TEAM: STRATEGIES

When you go to a game or watch a game on television, there are a few time-tested strategies that fans over the years have found work quite well. It starts with general rules that apply to all strategies:

1. Enjoy yourself—watching a hockey game is not work.

2. If you drink and then travel to a game, get a designated driver.

3. Watch a hockey game with people you like.

4. Learn as much as you can about the game of hockey.

5. Wear what you want, but hard-core fans wear jerseys.

THE TELEVISION STRATEGY

Most times, you cannot get to the game. It may be out of town or sold out or too far away or beyond your budget. But that doesn't mean you cannot enjoy the NHL. According to a non-scientific poll of some people in Massachusetts (conducted by my co-author), the four most important parts of a good television strategy are:

1. A television

2. Friends

3. Food

4. Beverages

Of course, this includes a number of assumptions: You have an antenna or cable or satellite dish of some sort; it's hockey season; there is a game being broadcast in your area. If this is all true, pop open a beverage and grab a handful of chips. Then watch the action because—wow, did you see that?!

 ## STARTING AS A HOCKEY FAN

The best place to learn the game is from up high where you can see the overall plays develop. The seats down low by the boards are good for sophisticated fans who want to see some of the intricacies like stickhandling. As you develop your knowledge of the game, you should move down to see other aspects of the game—especially speed and hitting.

On-the-Cheap Game Strategy

This strategy works best if you begin immediately after the previous season ends. Call the ticket office of your local team and find out when tickets go on sale for next season's games. Get a schedule and prices. Figure out what you can afford and then buy seats for those games as early as possible.

On game day, eat before you leave. When you go to the game, pack a snack, bring a drink for the ride, and then take public transportation if it is available. If not, don't fret about the parking prices. They are all usually about the same price (high or low, depending on the city) near the arena. It is okay to eat a little at the game, but remember, food prices can be high in major league arenas.

With-the-Family Strategy

Kids love souvenirs. Don't disappoint them. Plan ahead and set a budget. Your kids will remember the souvenirs 20 years from now. You may not want to buy something every time, but your kids will think even one souvenir is special.

For the rest of your family strategy, you can eat on the cheap side or expensively. Pizza parlors are usually located near downtown arenas. The game itself is entertainment enough for the kids. You may want to stick around afterward to try to get an autograph, although you should make it clear to your children that players probably cannot sign autographs for every child. The most important part of this and all strategies is to have fun.

On-the-Town Strategy

The National Hockey League is big-time entertainment and can cost you some big-time entertainment dollars. If you choose, you can really make a night of it. Almost all arenas are in the center of a city and therefore are near the classiest restaurants and coolest clubs anywhere. Go to an elegant restaurant before the game. After dining, go to the very best seats you can afford. While at the game, no matter where your seats are, you are expected to at least think like a hockey fan (Yaaaaaaargh!) even if you have to act like a civilized person in really nice clothes.

Afterward, go dancing. And if you want to really do it up in style, hire a limousine with champagne and roses to drive you around for the night.

With-the-Gang Strategy

Sometimes, you'll go to a game with the gang. These friends of yours are together to celebrate your friendship and frame it inside an NHL game. Going to a hockey game with a group of friends is exhilarating. Everybody pitches in for food and beverages and gas and anything else that is part of the shared expense. Then you appoint a designated driver and head on your way. In a group like this, although it's not a law, it is important for at least half the people to wear team jerseys.

 ## WINNING IS SHARING

I remember the year we beat Montreal in a playoff series for the first time in decades and arrived back at Boston's Logan Airport in the middle of the night.

There were more than one thousand wild and happy fans waiting for us! It was a fantastic feeling to know our actions on the ice had brought so many people so much happiness. It is still hard to describe that feeling. When fans show they care, it really hits home. I could only imagine what it would be like to win the Cup and have a parade in front of your hometown fans. We've all seen it on TV and I've heard from friends of mine who have won the Stanley Cup about what a great experience it is.

Learning to Play for Kids, Parents, and Coaches

Hockey is fun. Enjoy yourself. Whether you play, coach, or watch, somewhere along the way take a breath and remember that the competition is just plain fun. But it is competition and does involve skills.

This final part of the book is about the skills you need to succeed as a player. Here I will talk about the basics of skating skills, moving without the puck, moving with the puck, shooting, and goaltending. Finally, I will talk about maybe the most important of all skills in hockey—to play as the member of a team. I hope that, in this part, I teach something about a winning attitude. So enjoy yourself and believe. And, of course, have as much fun as possible. After all, hockey is fun.

13

Skating Skills

ome things are essential. In life, you need oxygen. In hockey, you need to know how to skate. Skating is not a skill that you can get by with by being merely adequate. You need to excel to play at a top level. You don't need to be able to skate like Pavel Bure of the Vancouver Canucks in order to play the game, but all players have mastered basic skills. When they combine skating skills with their other skills, good players become great players. Some players are considered good players because of their superb skating skills.

SKATES

When you start out, you need a sturdy skate with a lot of support. Many beginning skaters feel as if they are skating on their ankles. Good ankle support is crucial. You should be able to lace your skates up tightly without constraining your ankles. Then you can concentrate on skating. But all people are different. Keep adjusting your skates until you feel comfortable in them. Most skates are two sizes smaller than your usual shoe size, so be sure to try on skates in several sizes. My shoe size is 12, yet I wore 9-1/2 or 9-3/4 skates.

Skates need to be sharpened properly. When you skate on them, or when you look at them, you can tell if they are sharpened correctly. If your skates are too sharp, you are always catching an edge someplace you didn't intend. If they are not sharp enough, you fall a lot because you don't have an edge. You can also tell just by looking. Check your skate blades to see if there is an edge (see Chapter 3 for more about skates).

It's Not Walking

Ice is different from land, and skating is different from walking or running. Skating is not about stepping forward as much as it is about pushing back. Let the blade cut into the ice and push; that's how you get your stride. The push is the driving force. The push is not straight back but back and to the side. Your feet should be angled outward. This helps you get maximum thrust from the big muscles in your thigh.

Forward/Backward, Left/Right: Every Possible Way

Round and round, left and right, up and back, and then all over again in the other direction. As a player, you have to be ready to go any direction at any time. It is not enough to play in a straight line back and forth on one side of the ice, as in the old mechanical hockey game. That worked years ago when the game was more rigid and the positions were more defined. Hockey in the modern era is a free-flowing game, and it is played that way at all levels.

Going Forward

Forward is the most natural way to go on skates. It is the way you will skate most of the times: chasing the puck, keeping up with the puck, or chasing an opposing player. Although speed is important, a quick start is just as important. A player waiting for the puck to drop at a face-off should have one leg back and the other up a little bit with the blade turned out for a good strong push-off.

Skating requires balance and a strong push-off.

Skating involves more than just your legs. You need to swing both arms and your head needs to be up to see where you are going. The stride is very important too. Don't lift your legs up too high when you stride or you will waste energy. Be sure to finish the stride all the way back so that your knee is straight and your skate is at a right angle to your direction when you finish the stride. Remember, you are not running. You are pushing and gliding.

Going Backward

Sometimes you have to back up. An essential skill for hockey players is knowing how to skate backward. The key part of that skill is posture; it's almost like sitting in a chair.

Backward thrust works the same as forward thrust except for one main difference: Your knees only bend one way. In backward skating, you get your power by pointing your skates in, pushing off the blade, and shifting your weight from hip to hip.

Skating backward requires bent knees and a push forward with a slight side-to-side motion of your hips.

No Long Straight Lines

The shortest distance between two points in hockey is not always a straight line. Sometimes, you have to go around another player. Other times you have to stop and turn and go in a different direction. Players are always moving and looking for ways to get to where they want to go quicker and better than the opposing players.

 ## CHANGING DIRECTIONS

Hockey players are often called upon to go first this way, and then that way. When you skate, you will have to learn to make a pivot on one skate so that you can change directions quickly and cleanly.

The pivot is simple. Dig one skate into the ice and then swing your hips, shoulder, and free leg in the direction that you want to skate. Be sure that your free leg is up off of the ice enough so as not to catch. Then, when you put that leg down in a bent position, you will be in a position to immediately push off in your new chosen direction.

 ## GOTTA STOP

It is easy for beginning skaters to stop—they fall. Or they slam into the boards. As you learn to skate, you will also learn to stop. There are three common techniques for stopping.

Two-Bladed Stop

This is a classic stop and easy to learn. You have seen it a million times if you watch hockey. A player rushes down the ice and then suddenly leans back and stops on both skates as snow blows out in front of him.

The key to a two-bladed stop is to use both blades equally as you turn into the stop. Angle your skates into the ice in order to dig out a quick stop. Dig the inside edge of your forward skate into the ice and the outside edge of your back skate into the ice. Stay balanced and do not favor either side.

A two-bladed stop requires balance as you dig both blades into the ice at the same time.

One-Bladed Stop

When you use only one blade to stop, the other leg is free to begin to move in another direction. Of course, unless you master this technique, you can end up off-balance and unable to be effective. The one-bladed stop is usually done on the outside leg, but you can do it on the inside leg if you are able to maintain your balance.

A one-bladed stop gives you a split second of extra time to start to move in any direction.

 CROSSOVER

Hockey players have to be able to turn as they skate. The best way to turn is to cross your skates, one over another, in order to negotiate your way around a bend. Use your outside leg for power and push off. The final step of the crossover is to actually cross over, which is what you do with your outside leg after you push off—you cross that leg over in front of the other leg.

Backward Crossover

This is like a regular crossover. Use your outside leg and pull it inside of the other leg and then push off. This is how you turn when moving backward.

 ## IT TAKES TIME

All of these skills are easily learned and must be mastered. If you fall (and you will), get back up and try again. Every coach on every team will tell you that the more you practice, the better you will get at any skill. This is certainly true of skating.

Coach Dave Poulin's Drills

My former teammate with the Bruins is now the coach of the University of Notre Dame Hockey Team. Here are some simple drills Coach Poulin suggests to improve your skating skills:

THE UP-THE-MIDDLE WARM-UP

The idea of this drill is to work on using both sides of your skate blades so that you learn to get a natural feel of lightness on skates, almost like floating. Although the natural tendency of skating is to sink down into the ice, the goal of a good hockey skater is to get up almost off the ice. This drill demonstrates a number of ways to use both sides of the skate blade.

All players line up at one end of the ice by the net. Two players at a time head down the ice in a relaxed stretching mode. The real work is done between the Blue Lines. At the first Blue Line, the skater practices one of the following drills listed below. When the skater reaches the second Blue Line, he or she skates to the end and comes back along the boards. At the end of the ice, each player turns a different way to come back along opposite boards. Meanwhile, a new set of two players is skating down the middle. The middle part of the ice, from Blue Line to Blue Line, is where the work is done.

First, players should work on lengthening their stride by using the inside edges of both skates.

The next time down the ice, between the Blue Lines, players can work on doing three crossovers to the left, concentrating on the left side of each blade.

The next time down the ice, do three crossovers to the right, concentrating on the right side of each blade.

The next time down the ice, do three backward crossovers on one side. And then on the other side the next time down the ice.

All the work is between the Blue Lines. The rest is just stretching.

FULL CIRCLES BETWEEN THE BLUE LINES

This is a simple drill.

Go in circles at full speed and you will work on using your inside edges. Then turn and skate backward in a circle. The aim is not just to develop the physical skills of skating but also the mental confidence of skating well.

RUSSIAN CIRCLES

The crossover is an important skill and so is the lean when you turn. Learning to turn quickly in both directions is a key skill.

One player starts out on each of the five face-off circles and begins skating. Then, skating from circle to circle, the player skates around each circle in opposite directions. The aim is to work on turning and leaning in different directions. This is a great drill for improving body weight control.

THE MONTREAL STAR

This is a simple drill to learn to stop and go quickly. In this drill, four players are involved in a bit of a race.

All four players start in the center face-off circle, positioned in the four "corners" ready to go off in different directions. When the race starts, all four head to the nearest face-off spot, then back to center ice, and then back out to the face-off spot on their side that is near one of the nets. Since there are eight face-off spots, all four should have different spots to head to. When they are finished with one side, rotate until all four have gone off in all four directions. As players stop and turn, they should alternate the pivot skate so that they learn to stop on both skates.

14

Moving Without the Puck

Hockey is a game on ice—fluid, continual, flowing. Hockey stops and hits! Hockey is quick and fast, long and graceful, and there are a million indescribable things that a hockey player does during any one shift. A hockey player is always moving—with the puck, without the puck.

On offense, the idea is to create a target. On defense, the idea is to block the target. In normal time, that's simple logic. But hockey is played in hockey time. The game moves quickly and so must the players. Although only one player has the puck, all the players are moving.

 ## WHO HAS THE PUCK?

Possession in hockey is a funny thing. Offense and defense are not always as clearly delineated as they are in other sports. You have to constantly move offensively and defensively to keep up with the puck. Possession of the puck can switch, and switch, and switch again in the blink of an eye. Or it may not. You just never know what will happen next.

On Offense

Players have to keep up with the puck, then get ahead of the puck and break open into holes. The aim on offense, when you don't have the puck, is to be in a position to help the player who does have the puck. Get ahead to a place where the player with the puck can pass it, always looking to move into the open for a quick pass or a shot on net.

On offense, the idea is simply to get open.

It doesn't take long to score a goal. Therefore, the idea is not to be open for a long time, but to be open. The purpose of moving without the puck is to get to a place that is open, to be there at the right instant—the instant the puck gets there is the right instant.

The high guy plays farthest
from the net.

Where to Go? It's Up to You!

Do what feels right. Don't think too much. Figure it out and act at the same time. Except for the power play, there are no specific plays. Everything else is decided on the fly. As you play, you will learn to find openings. The more you skate and the more you play, the easier it will be to sense them. And, when you become even better, you can sense when they are about to develop.

When there is a breakout, try to move to an open spot. Go into a sort of lane where no one else is, and then move down the ice. This may mean at full speed, or it may mean going and stopping or turning. You have to flow with the game and make adjustments to the puck and the play—and the score.

When you are moving on offense, get to a place where a teammate can pass you the puck without shooting it past a number of defenders—the fewer the better. If you can, break into openings to give the player with the puck a chance to pass it to you without an opponent picking it off. You don't want the puck to be deflected. Help your teammates out with your ability to move without the puck. If you do, you will soon be moving with the puck (see Chapter 15).

If your team is winning, you will inevitably play conservatively (especially late in the game) so that you are better prepared to stop any scoring attempt against you. If you are winning, you don't need to score again as much as you need to stop the other team from scoring.

If, after you rush down, you are the last player in your offensive zone, you are the high guy—meaning you will play the farthest from the net, around the hatch marks up high in the slot.

You can switch positions, but someone always has to be high. If there is a turnover, that player is expected to get back first.

On Defense

When you play defense, you have to hustle. You must get back as fast as possible to pick up the next man and make sure you are in the right place defensively. The first player back on defense always takes the center position. When the center gets back, he fills the missing wing. Then the players will try to switch, but only when it is safe to do so. To switch, they yell "Switch!" or use some other prearranged signal.

Position is the key to defense. You are always trying to get in the proper position between a player and the net, with half an eye on the puck at all times. Moving and shifting is part of defense. You don't play a stationary position, you shift according to the puck and the opposing players.

Different strategies call for different specific actions by the team without the puck. In general, when your team does not have the puck, you cut off angles to the net. You have to think of not just the angle from the puck, but the angle to pass to other players and the angle that you are letting other players get to in front of the net.

Players on defense who are moving backward without the puck must be aware of opposing players getting in front of the net and in a position for a good shot on goal. On offense, I used to really work on getting in position in front of the net.

There is a certain rotation in front of the net. When your team is in your defensive zone, one defenseman is always stationed in front of the net. If the puck goes into the right corner, for instance, the right defenseman will chase it and the left defenseman will stay in front of the net. Both defensemen should never chase the puck into a corner.

No matter which corner the puck goes in, the center is usually there to help out the defenseman. Then, the strategy is generally for the first player to take the hit (or give the hit to an opposing player) from the other team. The second player's job is to get the puck.

If the puck moves to the other corner, the right defenseman will shift to the front of the net while the left defenseman goes in to dig it out and start something to move the puck to the other end of the ice.

Anticipation on Defense

Sometimes you will anticipate the play. This can work out as a quick turnover if you can get in the way of a pass at the right instant. Then you intercept the pass and break away. It's a great feeling. Sometimes, you get burned. You can go for a play and not get it. Then you are out of position and the other team has a quick advantage.

How do you decide? Trust yourself. Play a lot of hockey and learn from what works and what doesn't work. Remember, though, to take the score into consideration. If you are winning, there is no good reason to take a risk on a pass you aren't sure you can intercept. If you are up by a goal late in the game, you will play conservatively. But that doesn't mean playing scared hockey—instead, play smart hockey. If it is early in the game, you may want to take a chance.

 ## HITTING AND BODY POSITION

Generally, you need to have good body position on the opposing player to eliminate a pass or to keep him from getting a direct angle on the net. This means playing the body. You don't have to be big and strong and tough to play the body, but it helps. Contact is a big part of the game. There are some smaller guys in the NHL who play the body extremely well. These players have proven that no matter your size, you can play the body.

If you are going to play the body, keep your arms and stick down. Use your shoulders to make contact and keep your knees bent to maintain steadiness in your stance. In hockey, as in any contact sport, you will be hit and you will do some hitting. If you are a physical player, you're not always the one dishing out the body checks. So be ready for what's coming. I always say, though, that it's better to give than to receive.

Hitting is a big part of your job when you are moving without the puck.

Coach Dave Poulin's Drills

My former teammate with the Bruins is now the coach of the University of Notre Dame Hockey Team. Here are some simple drills Coach Poulin suggests to improve your skating skills:

THREE-SECOND SCRIMMAGE

To use a football analogy, all players should realize that when they do not have the puck, the player who does have the puck is the quarterback. Then all the other players are receivers. This three-second scrimmage is designed to make all players think like receivers.

It's like a regular scrimmage with one rule change: No player can keep the puck for more than three seconds at a time. This teaches players to move without the puck and to move into open space. The more you move without the puck, the better feel you will develop for the difference between where your eyes are and where the stick is. Your eyes may tell you that you are open, but your stick is not where your eyes are.

THREE-ON-THREE
BELOW THE TOPS OF THE CIRCLES

This drill is another way for players to learn to move without the puck. It is a regular scrimmage except when there is a change of possession. Then, rather than going the other way, the new team simply passes to a coach up top. The coach then makes the initial pass to start the offense for the new team in possession. This forces all players to initially move without the puck.

This also teaches the concept of "support" in which players make an effort to move toward the puck and support the player who needs to make a pass. Making the job easier for your teammates is part of moving without the puck.

Moving with the Puck:

Stickhandling

ontrol is a wonderful thing. When you have control of the puck and you are moving down the ice, you have the game in your hands for an instant. The focus is at the end of your stick. You should treat the puck at the end of your stick with a great deal of respect. When you have control of the puck, you feel it. It is a learned feeling that is more than just the stick and the puck touching each other. It is control through wrists, arms, and fingers—touch. When you are stickhandling, you are not pushing the puck, you are making it dance.

Stickhandling is touch. You know when the puck is on your backhand, and you can feel it on your forehand. You know where the puck is and you know how to make it do things. After a lot of practice, stickhandling is not a conscious effort; it becomes instinctive. Good stickhandlers have great instincts. They know how to move the puck. If you watch them, you can tell they know. Confidence has an aura. And all players know one thing—practice creates confidence.

ONE PUCK, ONE STICK: FIVE MILLION OPTIONS

Pass, stickhandle, move, shoot. It seems so simple and yet in the flow of a hockey game, every possible scenario of angles and human potential multiplies those four options. Suddenly, every moment is different. If you have the puck, you need to realize that the situation on the ice is changing by the microsecond. Thus, you must have control—absolute control. When you have the puck (this is very important), it is not enough to just have the puck. You want to own it. You want control.

Of course, the defense on the opposing team hopes you have no control. The defense would prefer you to be the defender and will probably do anything possible to bring about a role reversal. When you are on the defense, that's your hope too. It's always better to have the puck. If you have it, try to keep it. Besides the opponent's defense, the boards and time will prevent you from keeping the puck. You will only keep it for a short time. In hockey, that is a certainty.

Stickhandling the Puck

The stickhandle motion is side to side or front to back. It is a method of control that increases your chances to do something good with the puck. You control the puck with your stick while keeping it slightly in motion so that you are ready to do something with it as soon as you spot an opportunity. You want touch on your wrists and forearms—the feeling of absolutely knowing where the puck is at the end of your stick along with knowing that you can make it do anything you want whenever you want.

Stickhandling is a simple action. The idea is to use the stick to flick the puck slightly back and forth. The flicking is short and quick with a little turn of the wrist. The key is then to dance the stick up over the puck and drop it into a "catching" position—with the stick blade back. And then, the puck is flicked back the other way.

Stickhandling the puck is a skill that you must practice to master. The idea is to develop a feel, a touch.

Front to Back Is a Little Different

When you are stickhandling front to back, you can release your bottom hand from the stick briefly in order to give yourself a bit more extension. This can be very helpful. You can also use this technique to bait an opponent to go for a steal. Of course, if you are not very adept, the opponent may very well get the steal. As with all skills, you will get better with practice.

PASSING

There are a lot of ways to pass the puck. You can pass with a forehand to slide the puck along the ice. You can use the walls as another player and bank the puck. You can lift the puck with a flick of the wrist to get it airborne and then watch it land softly, right on the stick of a teammate.

Passing is an art. In order to be good, you need a repertoire of different passes. Some situations call for one kind of pass and others require something completely different.

Forehand Pass

The forehand pass is the most common pass, a sweeping motion that sends the puck sliding on the ice. Use it when the other team does not have a reasonable chance to intercept the puck. It is easy to make and to receive. The forehand pass is all wrists and forearms.

By using the wrists and forearms, the forehand pass should be easy to control.

Backhand Pass

The backhand pass is similar to the forehand pass except that it is done in reverse. A key point of the backhand pass is to keep the blade along the ice. Many players have a tendency to lift this pass. Although that may be a good idea sometimes, it usually is better to maintain control and let your teammate "catch" the pass as easily as possible. Keeping the puck on the ice allows this to happen.

A backhand pass requires keeping the blade along the ice in order to go against the natural tendency to lift it.

Getting Some Air

There will be times when you do want to lift the puck. An opponent's stick or skate may be in the way of a straight line between yourself and a wide-open teammate. In those cases, flick your wrists just a little in order to lift the puck a few inches off the ice as you send it on its way to your teammate. The idea is to have it land "soft," so that it slides right to your teammate. This may sound and look difficult but you can master it. When you first try, the puck may wobble and then roll when it lands. Don't worry, just practice.

Lifting the puck is an important skill. Some players are better at it than others, but everyone can be good enough to have some control over how the puck lands.

Lifting the puck over an obstacle such as a skate or a stick is a technique that will improve with practice.

CRISP PASSES

When you make a pass, make it a good, clean on-the-money pass to your teammate. The aim is to lead the player because chances are the player you are passing to is moving at a good clip. You don't want to put the puck at his skates. You want to put it right on his stick. Ideally, you should put it right on his stick so that he is immediately able to do something else with it—like shoot.

Consider the Distance

Obviously, distance counts. If you want to make a long pass, you clearly want to send it hard—put some mustard on it. You may have to get it up over an opponent's stick. There is a different dynamic to a long pass than a short one. When you are close to your target, you don't have to pass as hard.

Passing to an Area

It is good to get off a crisp pass if you can, but sometimes you have such a small window of time to get the pass off that you simply have to spot the uniform and pass. You may not always be able to pass just the way you practiced. Sometimes your body will be turned in the wrong direction or sometimes something will happen in an instant and you don't have time for a clear look. Although a perfect pass is good, a good pass doesn't have to be perfect.

Sometimes you can pass the puck in front of the net and a teammate will be there who can angle it into the net. This is not often planned, but it often works. I used to like to be the guy in front of the net waiting for such a pass.

Reading Your Teammates

Pay attention to your teammates. This is hard to understand at first, but you will quickly learn that all players have tendencies—things they like to do. When you know the tendencies of your teammates, you can help get them in position to do the things they like. This is often a leading pass, or a pass to the side that a player likes to shoot from, or maybe just knowing what to look for from a teammate when you have the puck. Knowing your teammates can make you a much better hockey player.

After You Pass

Go! As soon as you get rid of the puck, get into an opening so that it can be passed back to you. Even if you make a great pass, go! Unless the pass ends up in the net, it does no good to admire your work. *Gosh, I made a great play* is not a very productive attitude when the puck is still in play. If you sit and admire a pass, you will most likely get drilled by a nasty check or burned by a player skating past you. In either case, all your good work will be for nothing.

Coach Dave Poulin's Drills

My former teammate with the Bruins is now the coach of the University of Notre Dame Hockey Team. Here are some simple drills Coach Poulin suggests to improve your skills moving with the puck:

THREE-ZONE CHAOS

This drill involves a lot of players and plenty of pucks. The team is divided into three groups equal in number. Each group takes a zone: one from the Blue Line into the goal, one between the Blue Lines, and one from the other Blue Line into the other goal. Each player is given a puck and the chaos occurs one zone at a time. When "play" starts, the object for each player is to protect his puck and stay in the zone while disrupting the other pucks.

This is a drill that can even be done inside the face-off circles, with up to five players and pucks inside the circle. It can get interesting.

CONES

Cones are great tools for hockey players to learn to move with the puck. Many coaches like to give players patterns to skate. Others (such as Coach Poulin) like to give the players more freedom to create their own pattern around the cones.

ODD-NUMBER DRILLS

This is one of Coach Poulin's favorites. He divides his team into two groups on each bench and then sets up a scrimmage. He goes to one bench and yells a number and then goes to the other bench and yells a different number. The aim is to create mismatches and make the players think differently. Sometimes it will be a 5 on 4. But it could just as easily be a 7 on 2 or even a 10 on 1.

LOMBARDIS

Named after the famous football coach, Vince Lombardi (because this is like a football drill and Coach Poulin names all his drills), this is a great way to learn puck control.

Five players line up, each with a puck, on the goal line. The coach is in front, motioning the players to move forward, back, left, and right with the puck. It is a simple drill that helps develop concentration and quick reactions as well as stickhandling skills.

The Art of Shooting

ever on, never in. That's always been my saying. It means simply this: If you never hit the net, you are never going to score. Sure, you have to miss the goalie. But the first thing you must do is shoot in the right direction. Otherwise, your only chance is a ricochet off another player. It happens, but not often. If you want to score, the best way is to shoot at the target.

That's simple enough. Hockey is a wonderful and often complex game. At its core is a game that simply keeps score, one goal at a time. If you don't shoot, you don't score. If you don't shoot at the net, your chances of scoring aren't good.

If you try to be too precise in picking where you want to shoot the puck, you might take too long in getting your shot off. It could get blocked or deflected. Remember, if your shot gets on net, there could be a rebound. For your one shot, you could create two scoring opportunities—if there is a rebound.

When you do have time, though, you can be more precise. But hockey is a fast game, so more often than not you won't have a lot of time to shoot.

PRACTICE, PRACTICE, PRACTICE

Some hockey players have a natural ability to shoot. Those people need to practice. Some people don't have as much natural ability. They need even more practice. Every hockey player can benefit from practice because, especially around the net, hockey can be a game of inches. Shooting is a precise art that, in the reality of a game, is not something you have time to measure and figure. You see the shot, you take the shot.

Learning to see the shot, and then how and at what angle to take the shot, is something that comes from practice. The more you practice, the better you'll get. That's the way it is in everything and is especially true in hockey.

The reason is simple: During a game you need to be able to react and put the puck exactly where you want. The holes to shoot past a goalie are usually very small. The more control you can get with the puck, the better chance you have of getting the puck past the goalie and into the back of the net. And when you do, nothing is sweeter.

It is interesting. In practice, coaches generally get on you if you do not hit the net with your shots. Yet, that may be okay if you are working on hitting a certain corner from a certain angle. In practice, you are working on accuracy to a specific spot. If you just shoot into the center of the net to please the coach every time, you will not be helping your game. Most coaches understand this and will, in fact, encourage you to shoot for spots in practice. They will tolerate mistakes, as long as they see progress. But if you keep sending shots off the boards or off the glass (in other words, not into the net), you may be getting into a habit of missing. You don't want to do that in the game. It's a fine line. In practice, you want to work on all the spots and not be too concerned when you miss the net. Yet you want to establish good habits of getting it in the net. Never on, never in.

The slap shot requires great hand-eye coordination.

Slap Shot

The slap shot is pure excitement, and it is not the kind of shot you can use to surprise anyone. But when done right, it creates tremendous velocity on the puck. A good slap shot sometimes goes fast enough to go past the goalie, even though he knows it is coming. Or sometimes, a hard slap shot will bounce off another player's stick and get into the goal by luck. I like to think of this as creating your own

Try this technique: In all shots, practice looking at the net while knowing where the puck is without looking down at it.

luck. As I have said before, never on, never in. You have to shoot to score, and good things happen when the puck goes near the net. If you want the puck to go near the net with good speed, a slap shot will work.

It takes great coordination and more time to execute a shot that starts with a backswing. This alone makes it tough: When you start the backswing, you lose contact with the puck.

Here's how to shoot a right-handed slap shot step-by-step:

The key component is balance. Your left foot should be slightly in front of the right, and as you pull back on your backswing, your weight should shift to your back leg.

Spread your hands on the stick. Your right hand should be loose so that as you begin your backswing, it slides up the stick. As you begin to swing into the puck, your right hand slides back down the stick toward the blade.

The swing is really a rotation and a body-weight shift combined with a precise slapping of the puck. A perfect slap is one in which the stick hits the ice slightly before it hits the puck. Your right (bottom) hand must remain firm at this point. The stick snaps through the puck as it carries along the full momentum of your swing. The follow-through should finish with your body weight shifting from your back leg to your front. Your follow-through faces the goal.

Forehand Shot

This is the shot that starts with your stick on the puck. There is no backswing, although you do want to get the puck somewhat behind your body so that as you "sweep" it forward, you get some body shift and therefore some power. The best part of this shot is that you get great accuracy. One reason for this accuracy is that you don't need to spend all of your visual energy on the puck. You already have it. Instead, you can look at your target.

The forehand shot has some power and is accurate.

The finish of the forehand shot includes a body shift and a wrist snap and, at the end, your back leg pushes against the ice.

Flip Shot

If you are in close to the net and you can get your stick underneath the puck, it is sometimes good to simply flip it up into the air. This shot may not be powerful but it is quick and accurate. Start this with a very short backswing. Or,

The flip shot allows you get some air and be accurate.

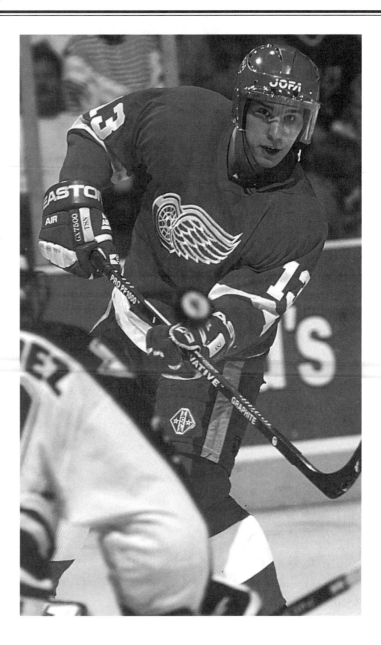

sometimes, there isn't even a backswing. It's just a flip of the wrist. The key is the quick wrist action that allows you to get your stick under the puck and then flip it right at the net.

The snap shot is quick and accurate.

Snap Shot

This is a shot that is similar to the forehand except that it does not include the sweeping motion. Instead, you start with the puck right in front of you and you snap your wrists—not to lift it as much as to launch it in a specific direction. Although this is not as powerful a shot as a slap shot, it can still be a hard, accurate quick shot. This makes it tough for goalies to stop.

The backhand shot is an important shot to add to your game.

Backhand Shot

Curved sticks have made the backhand shot a bit more difficult. The point of the curve is to gain more control for the more commonly used forehand shots. The motion of the backhand is very dependent on the action of the wrists, which provide all the control. Start similar to the forehand, with the puck slightly behind your body (and considering the direction you are shooting), and then pull the puck in a sweeping motion, shifting your body weight as you do.

The Release Point

One key aspect for any shooter to think about is the release point. Where, and when, does the puck come off your stick?

This is a great place to make adjustments in your shot. If you are missing a lot of shots, you obviously need to figure out why. For instance, if you are missing wide, you may be releasing too early. And if you are missing high, you may be releasing too late. You will know by the results and how the puck feels on your stick. You will know by practicing.

Rebounds

When the puck is shot, often the goalie will deflect it. It is best for the goalie if he smothers it or catches it. But for the scorer, a deflection is an opportunity for a rebound.

If you want to increase your chances of scoring, get in position for a rebound—this means standing in front of the net. To stand there, you will pay a price. Two defensemen will be battering you as best as they can and the goalie may also be reaching out with a stick or a glove to get you to go away. But, if you can put up with it, the chance for a rebound is worth the price. The actual rebound is simply a matter of hand-eye coordination. Find the puck and bang it back at the net.

Tip-Ins

A tip-in is a pass that is deflected into the goal. It is the kind of pass that goes from the full control of one player to, hopefully, the split-second full control of another player's stick. Bing, bing.

This sequence requires great hand-eye coordination and the stick movement by the shooter is minimal. It is not really even a shot. It's more of a redirection. And you can practice it.

CONTROL YOUR TEMPER

If you want to be a shooter, you will be taking some abuse in front of the net. The surest way not to score a goal is to get yourself into the penalty box. It's real tough to score sitting in there.

And, you must understand that when you get better, other teams will try to bait you. It is a common strategy to get a scorer out of a game. So, no matter what, keep cool. You'll help your team more from the ice.

Try this technique: A defenseman fires hard passes from the Blue Line to a forward positioned in front of the net. The forward can redirect it, tip it, knock it down, or deflect it toward the net. Although tip-ins are instinctive, any player can get better with practice.

 ## QUANTITY AND QUALITY

Never on, never in. That's one way to look at it. Another way is that if you put 50 shots from really easy positions, you are not really increasing your chances to score. I have seen teams with 17 shots on goals score more than teams with 50 shots on goal. Quality of shots are more important than the number of shots. Keep in mind that every time there is a shot, there is a chance for a rebound, and maybe the rebound itself will be the quality shot.

 ## STUDY THE GOALIE

Goalie's have tendencies. In the NHL, there is videotape and coaching and a wealth of information about every goalie. You may not have all of this information in your league, but you do have eyes.

Watch. Pay attention to your opponent and remember this goalie for the next time you get to play. If you see a goalie go down a lot, remember to give him a head fake low and try and go up high in one of the corners. If you see a goalie who doesn't do a good job of protecting the five hole between his legs, shoot the five hole more often than usual when you don't have time to think. When you are in the heat of a hockey game, you often will not have time to think. You will help yourself as a hockey player if you come prepared with some knowledge and a plan.

 ## KEEP LEARNING

You can always improve. Some people have a natural ability to shoot while others have harder time; every player can get better with practice. On a team, you get a lot of opportunity to practice shooting and you should take advantage of practice sessions.

You do want to score in practice. Although it is okay to miss at corners from time to time, success can become a habit. You always learn by playing. Every game, every practice, is part of your experience; the more you play, the more you see. Take the situations into account every time out on the ice. Don't just play—learn.

 ## SCORING

It feels great to score. It's fantastic. When the puck goes in and there is a reaction on the ice and in the stands, it is a feeling of accomplishment. All that work and now there are results.

Coach Dave Poulin's Drills

My former teammate with the Bruins is now the coach of the University of Notre Dame Hockey Team. Here are some simple drills Coach Poulin suggests to improve your shooting skills:

FIGURE 8 SHOOTING DRILL

In this drill, players are lined up in all four corners. A player comes out of each corner, skates around the closest face-off circle, receives a pass and shoots, and then skates in a completion of a figure 8 around the other face-off circle, receives another pass and shoots again. This goes on at all four corners so that there are always two pucks in play in front of both nets.

SHOOT AND GET

All the pucks in this drill are lined up at the goal line. All the players are in a semicircle up at the top of the circles. One players goes and gets one puck and then passes to any player in the semicircle who then shoots. After that player shoots, he goes and gets another puck and passes to another player (any player) in the semicircle. When a player makes the pass, he goes back to the semicircle of players.

THREE LINES EACH WAY FROM CENTER

This is a great shooting drill to get players to shoot from different angles. In this drill, all the players line up at either side of center ice, along the boards. Three players at a time leave that spot with a puck. This happens on each side, going toward each goal.

The first player heads right down the boards and then shoots from about 30 feet out. The next player goes across the ice to the other boards and then heads down the ice and shoots from that side from about 30 feet out. The third player is the control player. He doesn't go at full speed but rather does a little loop at center and then heads right down the middle and shoots from in closer.

Goaltending

oalies have to get comfortable facing shots. The key to learning how to be a goalie is to understand the job. Facing shots on goal is an integral part of the job description. When you play goalie, you have to have the guts and a desire to stand in front of flying pucks and do everything possible not to get out of the way. In fact, you must teach yourself to do the opposite of your instincts. When a hard object flies at high speed in the general direction of most humans, they will move out of the way. A goalie will smile and jump in the way.

At some time during their hockey lives, most players who are not goalies go into the net and play a little during practice. I know I did. It's intimidating! If you are not used being in net and you see a guy come down the ice and wind up for a slap shot—well, it's an interesting situation!

Being a goalie requires a different mentality. That's really the most important lesson you can learn if you want to play goalie. Sure, there are techniques, and we will talk about them in this chapter. But goaltending is attitude and instinct. You can develop both.

ATTITUDE—NOTHING GETS PAST ME

There is an end of the world for offensive hockey players. It is right in front of a great goaltender's net. The great goalies believe they are the best and it does not matter what kind of tricks or force the offense uses. Great goalies have confidence—*They can't get it past me.*

Attitude

I am not a goalie but I have shot against quite a few. When a goalie stops a shot that you think should have gone in, you can see their confidence grow. With some, it is a swagger. With others, it is quieter, yet no less of an aura. Goalies who are hot have a charisma of infallibility. It is a power. Confidence makes a goalie play better.

All athletes need confidence. Goalies need extra amounts of it. Confidence is not something that can be taught on a step-by-step basis. Yet, confidence may be the most important asset for a goalie to possess. You have to believe in order to stop a puck. You have to believe in order to bounce back from a goal (and if you are a goalie, you will eventually give up goals). You have to develop a thick skin, an overwhelming sense of self-confidence in your abilities and reflexes, and a sense of calm in the face of accelerating tension.

Intensity and Posture

Goalies need more than attitude—they need focus, an incredible intensity and vision. The intensity is an inner drive that forces you to focus and tense your muscles, ready to react to anything.

Goalies also need proper technique. Your stance should cover as much net as possible if you don't move, while giving you maximum flexibility to cover the rest of the net if you do move. Keep your glove hand down around your knees

A goalie should crouch and be ready for anything.

and your stick blade on the ice. Bend your knees and keep your arms out to your sides. Crouch and feel the intensity in every muscle. Be ready for action with muscles that have springs in them. Crouch and be ready to pounce—like a hungry cat.

USE YOUR PADS

As a goalie, you wear a bunch of big, fat pads. They are wider than the various parts of the body that they protect and can be used to block shots. Use them. The pads are wide and can be used almost geometrically to cut corners and angles. From time to time, you are going to take a puck in the body. Don't be afraid. Think of it as a job well done.

Double-Pad Slide

The purpose of this save is to stop absolutely everything low into the net. Throw your legs off in one direction with your bottom leg right along the ice. Stretch out your bottom arm behind you along the ice to cover low on that side. Keep your glove hand up to grab anything a little higher up.

The double-pad slide should cover just about the entire bottom half of the net.

The Butterfly

This move requires sliding your lower legs apart and to the sides while falling to your knees, bringing your knees together. Your arms should fan out like wings, ready to stop pucks aimed at the upper corners.

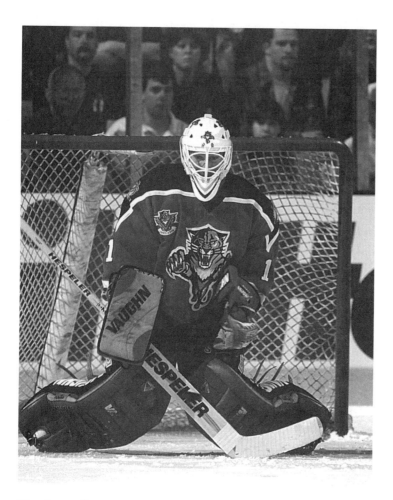

The butterfly save gives you a chance at getting to every corner of the net.

Glove work is a matter of reactions and hand-eye coordination. The better you get with your glove, the more it will help your goaltending.

 ## USE YOUR GLOVE

In order to best use your glove, first you have to know how good you are at using it. Then you can determine how much of the net you can, in essence, give to your glove hand. This is a very important consideration in determining little nuances of angle and position.

If you are good with the glove, you will inevitably believe you can cover more of the net with your glove. As a result, you will use your body to cover the other side of the net.

If you are not as good with your glove, you will inevitably believe that your glove hand would be better off covering less area of the net. As a result, you may shift your body slightly in that direction, thus giving up position on the other side.

Glove work is simple. It's in the eyes and the reactions. See the puck, catch the puck. Yes, it's simple until you do it. Then it is challenging.

 ## USE YOUR STICK

Goalies have a bigger stick than their teammates and should develop quick, deflecting skills with it. This is especially helpful for shots headed between your legs.

When the puck gets in near the net, you can also poke check the puck by reaching out with your stick and hitting the puck out of the opponent's control. It helps your team if you can act like an extra defenseman and actually make a pass up the ice to get a breakout started. The stick can also be used to freeze the puck off to one side or the other, or behind the net, until one of your defensemen can pick it up and begin taking it up the ice.

Goalies can help play a key part in getting breakouts started.

PLAY THE ANGLES

A goalie can come out away from the net, right at the player with the puck. When he does, he cuts the angle for the shooter. On first thought, this seems like a good idea. On second thought, the player with the puck isn't necessarily the shooter. He can pass. And if he does and the goalie is out away from the net, suddenly the new shooter has a great angle for a shot on goal.

Hockey games are fluid, always changing. Goalies need to keep this in mind as they look for the perfect angle. The situation that exists now can be completely different a few seconds from now. There is no perfect angle other than the evolving one.

Lateral Movements

Follow the puck, guard the net. That's the goalie's whole job. Those two little details combine to create a whole lot of lateral movement. As a goalie, you will move side to side, right in front of the net. You will most likely go from pole to pole. It's not a lot of motion, but it's very important. The movement is simply a pushing from side to side with the skates. The thought process is about angles, puck position, and the goalie's ability to use the equipment.

Cover the Short Side

When the puck is closer to one post, the goalie will always lean that way to keep that side of the net completely covered. If the puck is passed to the other side, the goalie should have enough time to slide to the other side to get the puck.

 ## RIDE THE GOOD, FORGET THE BAD

If you are a goalie, you need a thick skin. Every athlete learns to deal with failure—it is the nature of competition that somebody wins and therefore someone else loses. No one wins all the time. Goaltending is symbolic of all of that.

The spotlight in a hockey game is very bright upon the goaltender. As a goalie, remind yourself to learn from every goal you give up. Then, take every save and build on it. It's hard to explain, but I have seen goaltenders build an aura. Confidence is incredibly important in goaltending.

A goalie's attitude can rub off on an entire team. When a goalie is faltering and down on himself, the whole team feels it. When a goalie is on a roll and making great saves, the team feeds off his success. The pure confidence the goalie can transfer to the team often creates extra offense. A great save or two by the goalie helps the team out in more places than just the immediate effect on the scoreboard. Goalies sometimes play a sort of psychic offense.

When a goalie catches fire, his saves tend to fire up the entire team. Goaltender is the most important position on the ice, and all good goalies play as if they understand this crucial fact.

Coach Dave Poulin's Drills

My former teammate with the Bruins is now the coach of the University of Notre Dame Hockey Team. Here are some simple drills Coach Poulin suggests to improve your goaltending skills:

FAN-OUT

The purpose of goalie drills is to give the goaltender a look at as many different angles and different shots as possible. In the fan-out, players line up at opposite corners of the ice. A goaltender is in each net. Players at each end do this:

Three players at a time leave with pucks. The first player skates down the boards and then shoots. The second player skates to the Blue Line, crosses through to center ice, and then comes right up the middle and shoots. The third player skates to the Blue Line, crosses to the other side, and then skates down the other boards and shoots.

DOWN-LOW DRILL

In this drill, four players are set up near the goal. On each side of the net, one player is on the goal line and one is on the hatch marks. In a predetermined order, players on each side pass back and forth and set up different shots from different angles. For instance, the players along the goal line move toward the net and take shots from a side angle.

REBOUND GAME

This is a game between the goalie and five offensive players. You keep score up to 10. In this drill, one shooter is positioned with the puck up at the top of the circles. Two players are on either side of the net, creating a sort of "shooting alley." The game works like this:

If the goalie smothers the puck, he gets a point. If the puck hits the boards or if the goalie clears the puck to the boards, the goalie gets a point. Any other combination of shots and goals creates a point for the shooters.

18

Teamwork

Although it's a cliché, it's true: There is no "I" in the word team. Hockey is a team game. Players must understand early in their career that teams win championships. Everybody has to pitch in if the group is to prevail. After all, the other hockey groups want to win just as much as your team does. Hockey is a game of team dynamics. As a player, you either contribute or you take away. That's how team sports work.

When you are a team member, you play your role to the best of your ability in every game. While teams need stars, stars are not the only ones on the team. Every player has a role. Each team has different players with different roles.

THE SUM IS GREATER THAN THE STARS

Teams win hockey games. It is easy to point to any individual game and say that this player or that player won the game. But the reality is that the only way to win is when your team scores more goals than the other team. You can

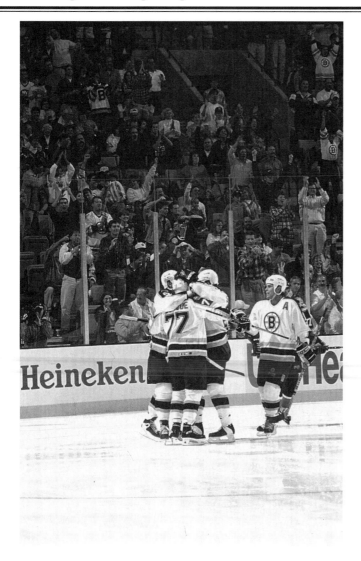

Teamwork means that everybody wins when something goes right.

think anything you want, but in hockey, it's one team versus another team. Teams also lose hockey games. Selfishness, a curse in any team sport, flourishes on losing hockey teams.

If you want to be a good team player (and if you don't, you probably shouldn't play a team sport), one of your biggest goals should be to make your teammates better. Try to make each team member's job as a hockey player easier. When you do, you will feel better about yourself and you will enjoy watching the results. It's a wonderful feeling to help a teammate. It's great for you and even better for the team.

Success is easier to achieve in a team sport when teammates play well together. This is more important than most young players realize. Being a team player doesn't have to mean making more passes, and it certainly doesn't mean skipping a chance for glory. Good hockey players play good hockey. And team hockey players play good hockey.

Every player plays a role on a team. My primary job was to score goals.

All good teams have stars, both in the NHL and in age-group leagues. It is the nature of organized sports. Teams have stars and that is good. And stars have a job—to play like stars. They know, more than anyone, that if they don't play like a star, they will greatly hurt the team. They also know that there is a team-mate just waiting for a chance to play like a star.

Every team has role players, and players should play their roles to the fullest. They are an integral part of the team; they are there for a purpose. It is, of course, very important for these players to work on all aspects of their game, but their role is to excel at one particular aspect. If they are supposed to be physical players, they should come out and play physical. Sure, they should chip in a goal from time to time, but these players that are brought in to take a body and bang and wear the other team down. Team play requires

Teams are full of camaraderie and players on the bench are always involved.

teammates to play to their skills. When that happens, the skills mesh into something more than the sum of the parts. There really can be magic! I hope all players get to experience the joy of playing on a real team.

ON AND OFF THE ICE: CAMARADERIE COUNTS

You don't have to be best friends to play well together as teammates, but you do have to understand each other and you have to be able to see a commitment from your teammate to work as hard as you do. When teammates understand each other enough to respect their differences and when they are willing to pay the price that it takes to succeed as teammates, something special happens. Much of it stems from off-ice talk. The talk may be personal or

Players can and should help each other.

it may be about hockey. Players get a sense of who cares and who doesn't. Everyone knows who acts like a teammate and who is on the team for some reason other than trying to win hockey games.

Sure, every team has coaches who teach and motivate the players. But sometimes players have to take charge of the results themselves. As a player, if you want to improve, you will have to call upon the player in the mirror to work harder, smarter, and with more of a lookout for his teammates. Being a team player first of all means being true to yourself—working your hardest, listening, and learning. Talk to teammates, watch them play, learn their strengths and favorite things to do. Winning hockey players spend some time thinking about hockey. Learn it, watch it, push yourself to learn more. The true joy of being on a team is going through the drama of athletics with a group of teammates. It's a shared experience. So have some fun and share your joy.

And then do one more thing, just for me. Even if you are a goalie, or just a fan, take a puck out on the ice and send a shot into the net. Go with a friend. Go on, try it. It's fun.

Coach Dave Poulin's Drills

My former teammate with the Bruins is now the coach of the University of Notre Dame Hockey Team. Here are some simple drills Coach Poulin suggests to improve your focus on teamwork:

TEN-ON-TEN WITH TWO PUCKS

Fun is an important part of teamwork. This drill is even more fun if you force every player to trade sticks with a player who shoots the reverse way. In other words, all right-handed shooters have to use a left-handed stick. This drill may not have a lot to do with specific hockey skills, but Coach Poulin has found the humbling experience of using the wrong stick is good as a morale builder. The idea is to remember that a team is all in it together. This drill is like a regular game but both pucks are live.

TWO-ON-TWO
ON A SHORT RINK WITH TWO PUCKS

In this drill, the nets are brought up to the Blue Lines so that the play is forced in close. Again, this is where decisions have to be made: Play offense or defense? There are two pucks! This drill brings a lot of fun to the ice.

SHOOTOUTS

Coach Poulin likes to make his college players do push-ups. In this drill, players wager their biceps on whether they believe a teammate will score in a penalty shot situation.

Everybody shoots. Before each shot, teammates guess whether that player will score or not. If you guess wrong, you have to do 10 push-ups. Some players have guessed wrong on every one of their teammates, according to Coach Poulin.

Team Addresses

Anaheim Mighty Ducks
Arrowhead Pond of Anaheim
2695 Katella Ave.
Anaheim, CA 92806

Boston Bruins
One Fleet Center
Suite 250
Boston, MA 02114-1303

Buffalo Sabres
One Seymour H Knox III Plaza
Buffalo, NY 14203

Calgary Flames
PO Box 1540 Station M
Calgary, Alberta T2P 3B9

Carolina Hurricanes
5000 Aerial Center Parkway
Suite 1000
Morrisville, NC 27560

Chicago Blackhawks
1901 West Madison Street
Chicago, IL 60612

Colorado Avalanche
1635 Clay Street
Denver, CO 80204

Dallas Stars
Dr Pepper Star Center
211 Cowboys Parkway
Irving, TX 75063

Detroit Red Wings
600 Civic Center Drive
Detroit, MI 48226

Edmonton Oilers
11230 - 110 Street
Edmonton, Alberta T5G 3G8

Florida Panthers
100 Northeast Third Avenue
2nd Floor
Fort Lauderdale, FL 33301

Los Angeles Kings
P.O. Box 17013
3900 West Manchester Blvd.
Inglewood, CA 90308

Montreal Canadiens
1260 de La Gauchetiere St. W.
Montreal, QC H3B 5E8

Nashville Predators
501 Broadway
Nashville, TN 37203

New Jersey Devils
50 Route 120 North
PO Box 504
East Rutherford, NJ 07073

New York Islanders
Naussaue Veterans' Memorial Coliseum
Uniondale, NY 11553

New York Rangers
14th Floor
2 Pennsylvania Plaza
New York NY 10121

Ottawa Senators
1000 Palladium Drive
Kanata, Ontario K2V 1A5

Philadelphia Flyers
1 Core States Complex
Philadelphia, PA 19148

Phoenix Coyotes
One Rennaissance Square
2 North Central, Suite 1930
Phoenix, AZ 85004

Pittsburgh Penguins
66 Mario Lemieux Place
Pittsburgh, PA 15219

St. Louis Blues
1401 Clark Ave.
St. Louis, MO 63103-2709

San Jose Sharks
525 West Santa Clara Street
San Jose, CA 95113

Tampa Bay Lightning
401 Channelside Drive
Tampa, FL 33062

Toronto Maple Leafs
60 Carlton Street
Toronto, Ontario M5B 1L1

Vancouver Canucks
800 Griffiths Way
Vancouver, BC V6B 6G1

Washington Capitals
1 Harry S. Truman Drive
Landover, MD 20785

Major NHL Trophies and Awards

Team Awards

The Stanley Cup: Given to the team that wins the championship of the NHL.

Prince of Wales Trophy: Given to the team that wins the Eastern Conference of the NHL.

Clarence S. Campbell Bowl: Given to the team that wins the Western Conference of the NHL.

Individual Awards

Hart Memorial Trophy: Given to the player judged to be the most valuable to his team.

Art Ross Trophy: Given to the player who has scored the most points at the end of the season.

Calder Memorial Trophy: Given the best rookie in the NHL.

James Norris Trophy: Given to the best defenseman.

Vezina Trophy: Given to the goaltender judged to be the best at his position.

William M. Jennings Trophy: Given to the number of goals for the season.

Frank J. Selke Trophy: Given to the forward who best excels at defensive aspects of hockey.

Lady Byng Memorial Trophy: Given to the player judged to exhibit the best type of sportsmanship and gentlemanly conduct combined with a high standard of playing ability.

Lester B. Pearson Award: Given to the NHL's Outstanding Player as judged by the NHL Players Association.

Conn Smythe Trophy: Given to the player judged to be the most valuable to his team during the playoffs.

Jack Adams Award: Given to the best NHL Coach.

Bill Masterton Memorial Trophy: Given to the player who best exemplifies the qualities of perseverance, sportsmanship, and dedication to hockey.

Lester Patrick Award: Given for outstanding service to hockey. Players, coaches, officials, executives, and referees are eligible.

Alka-Selzer Plus Award: Given to the player who, having played at least 60 games, leads the league in plus/minus statistics. This is calculated by giving a player a plus when he is on the ice and his team scores an even-strength or short-handed goal. The player receives a minus if he is on the ice when the other team scores an even-strength or short-handed goal.

King Clancy Memorial Trophy: Given to the player who best exemplifies leadership qualities on and off the ice, and has made a noteworthy humanitarian contribution in his community.

The Neely House at New England Medical Center

Caring for families. That's the mission of The Neely House, where everyone understands that some battles are a lot tougher than the ones waged out on the ice by hockey players.

The fight against cancer is obviously difficult for the patient. It is also difficult for the families of cancer patients who must wait and pray while their loved ones get care in a hospital. The Neely House is a place of comfort for families during the wait.

Cam Neely, his brother Scott, and his sisters Christine and Shaun know about the need for such a place all too well. They recently lost both parents to the disease, and the experience left them with a deep understanding of cancer's toll on families and how much support they need and should have while struggling to help loved ones through treatment. The Neely House was conceived through their own experience with the disease.

Located in the confines of New England Medical Center in Boston, The Neely House is a refuge for families of patients. It is more than just housing. It gives families the opportunity to talk with others facing similar situations while being near loved ones in a non-clinical setting. Social work services are available 24 hours a day to patients and their families.

"There needs to be a tremendous amount of money spent on research," says Cam Neely. "We know that, but we want to spend the money we raise to provide support directly to families dealing with this disease. We want to take some pressure off patients and families by giving them a safe and comfortable place to stay."

Scott Neely, executive director of The Cam Neely Foundation, adds, "Family members are very affected by a disease like cancer. They go through a difficult time just as the patient does. They need information and they need to feel included in the process of treatment and decision making. At New England Medical Center, I've seen that there is a lot of concern for the emotional support of families and patients."

Contributions can be sent to:

The Cam Neely Foundation
30 Winter Street, 2nd Floor
Boston, MA 02108
Phone: (617) 346-5900
Fax: (617) 451-7725

Index